Repent! How, Even if, President Trump was the Antichrist the Church Wouldn't Know It.

By Timothy Medsker

Repent! How, Even if, President Trump was the Antichrist the Church Wouldn't Know It.

Cover Photo: President Trump, 2018, Missoula, Montana Photo from Brando Schuchardt, used with permission.

All Scripture taken from the VW Edition (www.a-voice.org), with permission.

www.allwillstand.org

First Edition

ISBN 978-0-9906958-7-5

"Now learn this parable from the fig tree: When its branch has already become tender and puts forth leaves, you know that summer is near." Matthew 24:32

Repent! How, Even if, President Trump was the Antichrist the Church Wouldn't Know It.

Contents		Page

Preface

The original material for this book was written in December 2019 & January 2020, prior to the removal of normalcy from the world, of which I am thankful for that.

With such a distraction that COVID-19 has become in our daily lives, I pondered the timing of the book back when it was published in January 2020. Certainly I would not have wanted the book to become skewed with thoughts of the current situation on my mind.

In October of 2020 a bonus chapter was written and added to the ministry's website (www.AllWillStand.org). This update to that book includes that chapter *The End is Near*. In this chapter the argument is made based upon biblical prophecy of why President Trump MUST be a suspect of being the Antichrist. This is not my opinion, this is based upon what the Bible clearly states.

Now let me emphasize that this still doesn't mean that President Trump is the Antichrist. As this is being written in late December 2020, the election is still being contested by President Trump. I do not know the future, but logically it would seem that if President Trump is no longer in power, this would remove him from being a suspect, though the prospect of him rerunning in 2024 remains an open question.

Regardless of how the future plays out, one thing is certain. Whether or not President Trump remains a suspect of being the Antichrist or not matters little. The simple fact that he can be used as an example of how the Antichrist could rise to power and the church would seemingly not notice it, provides ample evidence of how such a thing could happen.

To my Baptist friends, particularly those who are independent, fundamental Baptists, I would ask you a question based upon a premise that you have. You have a correct premise that the Antichrist will come out of Rome, many thinking of the European Union. Well, where is Rome?

To that effect I would direct you to the other person who is behind All Will Stand's ministry and that is Brandon Schuchardt. He has written an excellent article entitled *The Night is Far Spent* (Chapter 7). That article is readily available on the website.

To close, much could be said about how COVID-19, immunity certificates, etc., could be preparing the world for the mark of the Beast *(Rev. 13:16)* or even perhaps become the mark of the Beast during the *"time of Jacob's trouble" (Jer. 30:7)*, better known as the Tribulation. Yet the scope of this book is not about that, though check the website for possible articles or radio shows about such subjects, as the Lord may lead.

Certainly with the condition of the world, if there was ever a time in the history of mankind to be watching and ready *(Luke 12:37-40)*, this would be it. I don't suppose to have all of the answers, nor can any man, but we do have what we need and that is God's

Word to mankind, the Holy Scriptures. This is the only absolute truth, provided we have a good translation like the King James Version, that we can know for sure.

Our goal as Believers is not to search for the Antichrist, but to preach the Gospel that people might be Saved. Nonetheless, when a man is rising to power, like Donald Trump, it should certainly be pointed out that he matches the characteristics laid out regarding prophecy about the Antichrist. The update to this book includes this preface and that bonus chapter, other than that the book remains the same.

Seek God before it is too late!

"And you shall seek Me and find Me, when you search for Me with all your heart." Jeremiah 29:13

"For He says: In an acceptable time I have heard you, and in a day of salvation I have helped you. Behold, now is the accepted time; behold, now is the day of salvation." 2nd Corinthians 6:2

Tim Medsker
December 24, 2020

For more information: **www.AllWillStand.org**

The Antichrist

"Let no one deceive you by any means; for that Day will not come unless the falling away comes first, and the man of sin is unveiled, the son of perdition, who opposes and exalts himself above all that is called God or that is honored, so that he sits as God in the temple of God, declaring of himself that he is God. Do you not remember that when I was still with you I told you these things? And now you know what is restraining, that he may be unveiled in his own time. For the mystery of lawlessness is already at work; only He is now restraining, until it is raised from out of the midst. And then the lawless one will be unveiled, whom the Lord will consume with the breath of His mouth and destroy with the brightness of His coming. The coming of the lawless one is according to the working of Satan, with all power, signs, and lying wonders, and with all unrighteous deception among those who are perishing, because they did not receive the love of the truth, that they might be saved. And for this reason God will send them strong delusion, that they should believe the lie, that they all may be judged who did not believe the truth but had pleasure in unrighteousness." 2nd Thessalonians 2:3-12

In this late hour there should be some preaching about the Rapture, the Antichrist, the Tribulation *("time of Jacob's trouble" Jer. 30:7)*, the Two Witnesses, the False Prophet, as well as the Great White Throne Judgment, where whoever has not repented and believed into Jesus Christ as their Lord and Savior will be cast into the Lake of Fire for all of eternity! These are very serious times, these are very serious issues.

"And the devil, who led them astray, was cast into the Lake of Fire and brimstone where the beast and the false prophet are. And they will be tormented day and night forever and ever. And I saw a great white throne and Him who sat on it, from whose face the earth and the heavens fled away. And there was found no place for them. And I saw the dead, small and great, standing before God. And books were opened. And another book was opened, which is the Book of Life. And the dead were judged according to their works, out of the things which were written in the books. And the sea gave up the dead who were in it, and Death and Hades delivered up the dead who were in them. And they were judged, each one, according to their works. And Death and Hades were cast into the Lake of Fire. This is the second death. And anyone not found written in the Book of Life was cast into the Lake of Fire." Revelation 20:10-15

A generation ago, back into the late 1990's there was still preaching going on about prophetic events that would take place in the future. The Bible is certain and while we will never be able to figure out all of the details, there certainly are enough details to fill multiple sermons on such subjects. Of course, would not the 'things to come' be a predecessor for answering the people why (they need to repent and believe the Gospel), as well as a stern warning for Believers to be carrying out the Great Commission until the Rapture happens?!

"Beloved, I now write to you this second epistle (in both of which I stir up your pure minds by way of reminder), that you may remember the words which were spoken before by the holy prophets, and the commandment of us, the apostles of the Lord and Savior,

knowing this first: that scoffers will come in the last days, walking according to their own lusts, and saying, Where is the promise of His coming? For since the fathers fell asleep, all things continue as they were since the beginning of creation. For of this they are willfully ignorant: that by the Word of God the heavens were of old, and the earth standing out of water and in the water, by which the world that then existed perished, being flooded with water. But the heavens and the earth which are now preserved by the same Word, are reserved for fire until the day of judgment and destruction of ungodly men. But, beloved, do not be unaware of this one thing, that with the Lord one day is as a thousand years, and a thousand years as one day. The Lord is not slow concerning His promise, as some count slowness, but is longsuffering toward us, not purposing that any should perish but that all should come to repentance. But the day of the Lord will come as a thief in the night, in which the heavens will pass away with a loud noise, and the elements will be dissolved with intense burning; both the earth and the works that are in it will be burned up. Therefore, since all these things will be dissolved, of what sort ought you to be in holy behavior and godliness, looking for and earnestly hastening unto the coming of the Day of God, through which the heavens will be dissolved, being set on fire, and the elements will melt with intense burning? Nevertheless we, according to His promise, look for new heavens and a new earth in which righteousness dwells. Therefore, beloved, looking forward to these things, be diligent to be found by Him in peace, spotless and without blemish; and consider that the longsuffering of our Lord is salvation; as also our beloved brother Paul, according to the wisdom given to him, has written to you, as also in all his epistles, speaking in them of these things, in which are some things hard to understand, which the unlearned and unstable twist, as they do also the rest of the Scriptures, to their own destruction. You therefore, beloved, since you know this beforehand, beware also that you not be led away with the error of the wicked, and *fall from your own steadfastness. But grow in the grace and knowledge of our Lord and Savior Jesus Christ. To Him be the glory both now and forever. Amen." 2nd Peter 3*

"And Jesus came and spoke to them, saying, All authority is given to Me in Heaven and on earth. Go therefore and instruct all the nations, immersing them into the name of the Father and of the Son and of the Holy Spirit, teaching them to observe all things whatever I have commanded you; and lo, I am with you always, even to the end of the age. Amen." Matthew 28:18-20

Our job as Believers is not to try and guess who the Antichrist may or may not be. Though I would say that if someone seems to fit the bill, based about characteristics of the Antichrist that the Bible clearly states, one should at least point out that in this late hour, someone who is seemingly matching the qualifications could possibly be it, as no one is paying attention! So even if the Antichrist was beginning to rise in power in our day and age, there is very, very few who would be paying attention, once again fulfilling prophecy!

"But know this, that in the last days perilous times will come: For men will be lovers of themselves, lovers of money, boasters, proud, blasphemers, disobedient to parents, unthankful, unholy, without natural affection, unyielding, slanderers, without self-control, savage, despisers of good, traitors, headstrong, haughty, lovers of pleasure rather than

lovers of God, having a form of godliness but denying its power. And from such people turn away." 2nd Timothy 3:1-5

"Now learn this parable from the fig tree: When its branch has already become tender and puts forth leaves, you know that summer is near. So you also, when you see all these things, know that it is near, at the doors. Truly, I say to you, this generation will by no means pass away till all these things are fulfilled. Heaven and earth will pass away, but My Words will by no means pass away. But of that day and hour no one knows, not even the angels of Heaven, but My Father only. But as the days of Noah were, so also will the coming of the Son of Man be. For as in the days before the flood, they were eating and drinking, marrying and giving in marriage, until the day that Noah entered into the ark, and did not realize until the flood came and took them all away, so also will the coming of the Son of Man be. Then two will be in the field: one is taken and the other is left. Two will be grinding at the mill: one is taken and the other is left. Watch therefore, for you do not know what hour your Lord comes." Matthew 24:32-42

Our world is a mess, violence fills our streets, drug abuse is rampant, the world economics are a house of cards, situated by the elite banksters, just waiting to come crashing down. There are wars and rumors of wars *(Matt. 24:6)*. The church is in shambles, the false doctrines and false christianity being preached has no end. The Churches that are holding out and being faithful to Christ are becoming less and less, as more and more Churches topple to the apostasy.

"But there were also false prophets among the people, even as there will be false teachers among you, who will secretly bring in destructive heresies, even denying the Lord who bought them, and bring on themselves swift destruction. And many will follow their destructive ways, through whom the way of truth will be blasphemed. By covetousness they will exploit you with well-turned words; whose judgment of old is not idle, and their destruction does not slumber. For if God did not spare the angels who sinned, but cast them down to Tartarus and delivered them into chains of darkness, to be reserved for judgment; and did not spare the ancient world, but saved Noah, one of eight people, a preacher of righteousness, bringing the flood on the world of the ungodly; and turning the cities of Sodom and Gomorrah into ashes, condemned them to destruction, making them an example to those intending to live ungodly; and delivered righteous Lot, who was oppressed by the lustful behavior of the wicked (for that righteous man, dwelling among them, his righteous soul was tormented from day to day by seeing and hearing their lawless deeds); then the Lord knows how to deliver the godly out of temptations and to reserve the unjust for the day of judgment, to be punished, and especially those who walk according to the flesh in the lust of defilement and despise authority. They are presumptuous, self-willed. They are not afraid to speak evil of dignitaries. Whereas angels, who are greater in power and might, do not bring a reviling accusation against them before the Lord. But these, like natural brute beasts made to be caught and destroyed, speak evil of the things they do not understand, and will utterly perish in their own corruption, and will receive the wages of unrighteousness, as those who consider it pleasure to carouse in the daytime. They are spots and blemishes, delighting in their own deceptions while they feast with you, having eyes full of adultery and that cannot cease

from sin, enticing unstable souls; having a heart exercised in covetousness; accursed children. They have forsaken the right way and gone astray, following the way of Balaam the son of Beor, who loved the wages of unrighteousness; but he was rebuked for his iniquity: a dumb donkey speaking with a man's voice restrained the madness of the prophet. These are wells without water, clouds being driven by a tempest, for whom is reserved the blackness of darkness forever. For when they speak great swelling words of vanity, they allure through the lusts of the flesh, through wantonness, the ones who have actually escaped from those living in error. While they promise them liberty, they themselves are slaves of corruption; for by whom a person is overcome, by him also he is brought into bondage. For if, after they have escaped the defilements of the world through the full true knowledge of the Lord and Savior Jesus Christ, they are again entangled in them and overcome, the end is worse for them than the beginning. For it would have been better for them not to have known the way of righteousness, than having known it, to turn from the holy commandment delivered to them. But it has happened to them according to the true proverb: A dog returns to his own vomit, and, a sow, having been washed, to her wallowing in the mire." 2nd Peter 2

"And to the angel of the church of the Laodiceans write, These things says the Amen, the Faithful and True Witness, the Beginning of the creation of God: I know your works, that you are neither cold nor hot. I would that you were cold or hot. So then, because you are lukewarm, and neither cold nor hot, I will vomit you out of My mouth. Because you say, I am rich, have become wealthy, and have need of nothing; and do not know that you are wretched and miserable and poor and blind and naked; I counsel you to buy from Me gold refined in the fire, that you may be rich; and white garments, that you may be clothed, that the shame of your nakedness may not be revealed; and anoint your eyes with eye salve, that you may see. As many as I love, I rebuke and chasten. Therefore be zealous and repent. Behold, I stand at the door and knock. If anyone hears My voice and opens the door, I will come in to him and dine with him, and he with Me. To him who overcomes I will grant to sit with Me on My throne, as I also overcame and sat down with My Father on His throne. He who has an ear, let him hear what the Spirit says to the churches." Revelation 3:14-22

The world is ripe for deception, in this chapter a study of characteristics of the Antichrist are going to be looked at, some will have possible theories provided, others are more certain. No one is going to know everything before the time happens, but those who are truly Saved will be Raptured out of here before the start of the Tribulation and the Antichrist being unveiled.

"For God did not appoint us to wrath, but to obtain salvation through our Lord Jesus Christ,"... 1st Thessalonians 5:9

"For if we believe that Jesus died and rose again, even so God will bring with Him those who sleep in Jesus. For this we say to you by the Word of the Lord, that we who are alive and remain until the coming of the Lord will by no means precede those who are asleep. For the Lord Himself will descend from Heaven with a shouted command, with the voice of the archangel, and with the trumpet of God. And the dead in Christ will rise first.

Then we who are alive and remain shall be caught up together at the same time *with them in the clouds to meet the Lord in the air. And thus we shall always be with the Lord. Therefore encourage one another with these words." 1st Thessalonians 4:14-18*

"After these things I looked, and behold, a door having been opened in Heaven. And the first voice which I heard was like a trumpet speaking with me, saying, Come up here, and I will show you things which must take place after these things." Revelation 4:1

First, understand that the Antichrist will not be unveiled until after the Rapture, so while some might suspect a person or a person might fit the bill, the proof of that will not be given until AFTER the Rapture happens, not before. So it is NOT possibly to say with certainty exactly who the 'man of sin' is.

There has been a lot of suspects throughout the years. There were those who suspected Bill Gates, Prince William, President Obama, President Clinton and many Popes. Personally when I was younger I found some of the information to be interesting, but never bought into any of those people being the Antichrist. Oddly, the only person who I have ever pondered about, due to fitting much of the characteristics listed in the Bible, is also extraordinarily rare to have anyone list him as a suspect. Nonetheless, the Bible is quite clear that the Antichrist is not unveiled before the Rapture.

"And then the lawless one will be unveiled, whom the Lord will consume with the breath of His mouth and destroy with the brightness of His coming." 2nd Thessalonians 2:8

There are a lot of misconceptions about the Antichrist, while not expecting to provide all of the answers here, perhaps a bit of insight into what the Bible teaches. I've looked around online at some of the resources out there, even looking at King James Version (KJV) only lists of Bible verses about the Antichrist and find that all of them fall short. This is not to say that there is not accurate information here and there, but a quick Google search reveals the ignorance of the times. A lot of what is written is extra biblical or simply pure garbage, often mixed with occultic works. I don't recommend believing much of what is read, but rather use the Bible as the sole authority and see if those things are so *(Ac. 17:11)*.

Antichrist is a Literal Person, an Individual, not Simply Possessed by Satan

First of all the Antichrist is a -literal- person who will rise to the scene. The Bible quite clearly prophecies this.

"Will you still think to say before him who slays you, I am God? But you are a man, and not a god, in the hand of him who slays you." Ezekiel 28:9

"He magnified himself even to the Prince of the host. And the regular sacrifice *was taken away by him, and the foundation of His sanctuary was cast down." Daniel 8:11*

"And he shall confirm a covenant with many for one week. And in the middle of the week he shall cause the sacrifice and the grain offering to cease. And on a corner will be abominations that cause horror, even until the end. And that which was decreed shall be poured out on the desolate." Daniel 9:27

"And forces will stand for him, and they will profane the sanctuary fortress. And they shall remove the regular sacrifice, and they will place there the abomination that causes horror." Daniel 11:31

"Therefore when you see the abomination of desolation, spoken of by Daniel the prophet, standing in the holy place (whoever reads, let him understand), then let those who are in Judea flee into the mountains. Let him who is on the housetop not go down to take anything out of his house. And let him who is in the field not go back to get his clothes. But woe to those who are pregnant and to those who are nursing babies in those days! And pray that your flight may not be in winter or on the Sabbath. For then there will be great affliction, such as has not been since the beginning of the world until this time, no, nor ever shall be. And unless those days were shortened, no flesh would be kept safe alive; but for the elect's sake those days will be shortened. Then if anyone says to you, Look, here is the Christ; or, There; do not believe it. For false christs and false prophets will arise and show great signs and wonders to lead astray, if possible, even the elect. Behold, I have told you beforehand. Therefore if they say to you, Behold, He is in the desert, do not go out; or, Behold, He is in the inner rooms, do not believe it. For as the lightning comes out of the east and flashes to the west, so also will the coming of the Son of Man be. For wherever the carcass is, there the eagles will be gathered together. And immediately after the affliction of those days the sun will be darkened, and the moon will not give its light; the stars will fall from heaven, and the powers of the heavens will be shaken." Matthew 24:15-29

"Let no one deceive you by any means; for that Day will not come unless the falling away comes first, and the man of sin is unveiled, the son of perdition, who opposes and exalts himself above all that is called God or that is honored, so that he sits as God in the temple of God, declaring of himself that he is God." 2nd Thessalonians 2:3-4

"And the devil, who led them astray, was cast into the Lake of Fire and brimstone <u>where the beast and the false prophet are</u>. And they will be tormented day and night forever and ever." Revelation 20:10

Clearly the Antichrist is a person who achieves actual things. This notion that there simply a spirit of antichrist and that there will never be a real Antichrist is not biblical. In Revelation 20:10 you can clearly see that both the beast (Antichrist) and the False Prophet are in the Lake of Fire, but Satan is not yet in the Lake of Fire, not for a thousand years after (Rev. 20:7)

Antichrist is Called both the Little Horn and the Beast

"I was contemplating the horns. And behold, another little horn came up among them, and three of the first horns were uprooted before it. And behold, in this horn were eyes like the eyes of a man, and a mouth speaking great things." Daniel 7:8

"And out of one of them came a little horn which became very great, toward the south, and toward the east, and toward the beautiful land." Daniel 8:9

"Then I stood on the sand of the sea. And I saw a beast rising up out of the sea, having seven heads and ten horns, and on his horns ten crowns, and on his heads names of blasphemy. And the beast which I saw was like a leopard, his feet were like the feet of a bear, and his mouth like the mouth of a lion. And the dragon gave him his power, his throne, and great authority. And I saw one of his heads as if it had been mortally wounded, and his deadly wound was healed. And all the world marveled at the beast. So they did homage to the dragon who gave authority to the beast; and they did homage to the beast, saying, Who is like the beast? Who is able to make war with him? And he was given a mouth speaking great things and blasphemies, and he was given authority to continue for forty-two months. And he opened his mouth in blasphemy against God, to blaspheme His name, His tabernacle, and those who dwell in Heaven. And it was granted to him to make war with the saints and to overcome them. And authority was given him over every tribe, tongue, and nation. And all who dwell on the earth will do homage to him, whose names have not been written in the Book of Life of the Lamb slain from the foundation of the world. If anyone has an ear, let him hear." Revelation 13:1-9

The Antichrist is called the 'little horn' in the book of Daniel and the beast in the book of Revelation. Both are speaking of the same person.

The Source of the Antichrist's Power is Satan

"The coming of the lawless one is according to the working of Satan, with all power, signs, and lying wonders,"... 2nd Thessalonians 2:9

"So they did homage to the dragon who gave authority to the beast; and they did homage to the beast, saying, Who is like the beast? Who is able to make war with him?" Revelation 13:4

Who knows what signs and lying wonders will take place regarding the Antichrist, but the power behind whatever the signs might be are the workings of Satan.

The Antichrist will have a Fierce Countenance and Understand Sinister Schemes

"And in the latter time of their kingdom, when the transgressors have come to the full, a king shall stand forth, having fierce countenance and understanding sinister schemes." Daniel 8:23

fierce, a.

1. Vehement; violent, furious; rushing; impetuous; as a fierce wind.
2. Savage; ravenous, easily enraged; as a fierce lion.
3. Vehement in rage; eager for mischief; as, a fierce tyrant; a monster fierce for blood.
4. Violent; outrageous; not to be restrained.
5. Passionate; angry; furious.
6. Wild; staring; ferocious; as, a fierce countenance.
7. Very eager; ardent; vehement; as, a man fierce for his party.

countenance, n.

1. The face; the visage, particularly as denoting the emotions; as, a man of goodly countenance.
2. Manifestation of regard; favor; good will; kindness; as to give one's countenance to graft.
3. Show; resemblance; appearance. (Obs.)

Webster's University Dictionary Unabridged, 1942

What exactly consists of a fierce countenance? When I consider a fierce countenance, I would believe that it would be a man who you would not mess with. Would the fierce countenance always be at hand or would it just come out during moments of anger?

From my perspective and my thoughts regarding understanding sinister schemes, is someone who would understand what goes on behind the scenes of the world, around the world. Just as Henry Ford tried to stop World War 1, because he understood what was going on behind the scenes, verses the public perception, so too, I would ponder whether or not this man, the Antichrist, would understand the new world order, the deep state, the 'powers that be' *(Eph. 6:12).*

..."also of the ten horns that were *on its head, and the other which came up, and before whom three fell, even that horn that* had *eyes, and a mouth speaking great things, whose appearance* was *greater than his fellows." Daniel 7:20*

I suppose that the appearance greater than his fellows will be something that will make sense at the time. If a group of world leaders were in a room together, would the Antichrist be someone who is distinguished as greater than those with him through looks, intelligence, character or something else?

The Antichrist's Rise to Power

"And I saw one of his heads as if it had been mortally wounded, and his deadly wound was healed. And all the world marveled at the beast. So they did homage to the dragon who gave authority to the beast; and they did homage to the beast, saying, Who is like the beast? Who is able to make war with him?" Revelation 13:3-4

There is some sort of supernatural miracle that occurs with the Antichrist. This is a deception of Satan, one of the signs and lying wonders. Does this set the stage for the Antichrist to declare himself as God?

One of the definitions of mortal is the following:

Deadly; destructive to life; causing death, or certain to cause death; as, a mortal would; mortal poison.

Webster's University Dictionary Unabridged, 1942

What seems to be indicated here is the Antichrist should be dead, but the wound is healed. The whole world would not marvel at the beast if the there wasn't a clear miracle here. This is one of the things regarding the Antichrist's rise to power. Whether or not it is an assassination, accident, what the mortal (deadly) wound is, the Bible does not say.

"And he shall confirm a covenant with many for one week. And in the middle of the week he shall cause the sacrifice and the grain offering to cease. And on a corner will be abominations that cause horror, even until the end. And that which was decreed shall be poured out on the desolate." Daniel 9:27

The Antichrist will confirm a peace pact with Israel. Clearly the Bible indicates that the peace deal is for 7 years. This is primary why Bill Clinton (aside from being President of the United States in the year 2000) was considered a suspect by many, because there was a treaty signed with Israel.

Perhaps the peace deal will be a two state solution *(Da. 11:39)*?

Yet, for all of those who decide they can live like the devil today and turn around at the last minute when they see the 'proof' of things, through a peace treaty with Israel...take heed!

"Then the kingdom of Heaven shall be likened to ten virgins who took their lamps and went out to meet the bridegroom. And five of them were wise, and five foolish. Those who were foolish took their lamps and took no oil with them, but the wise took oil in their vessels with their lamps. But while the bridegroom was delayed, they all nodded and fell asleep. And at midnight there was a cry: Behold, the bridegroom is coming; go out to meet him! Then all those virgins arose and prepared their lamps. And the foolish said to the wise, Give us some of your oil, for our lamps are going out. But the wise answered, saying, No, lest there should not be enough for us and you; but go rather to those who sell, and buy for yourselves. And while they went to buy, the bridegroom came, and those who were ready went in with him to the wedding feast; and the door was shut. Afterward the other virgins came also, saying, Lord, Lord, open to us! But he answered and said, Truly, I say to you, I do not know you. Watch therefore, for you know neither the day nor the hour in which the Son of Man comes." Matthew 25:1-13

Many were saying that we had entered the Tribulation during that time period. Well 2007 has come and gone. I've even known a woman who was a candidate for the House of Representatives who stated that we were in the Tribulation, this back in 2008, be not deceived! The Oslo Accords were signed in secret BEFORE being made public.

Let me ask you, when this ultimate deal is made, is it not confirmed, done in meetings, agreed upon, before the paper is signed? Who signs to purchase a home, unless the decision has already been made? A signature, even a public signing, is something that is agreed upon -prior- to the ink being placed on the paper. Do not suppose that you have time to run and 'get oil' once you hear of it, for the Rapture might very well have already taken place. Do not mess with your eternal destination and postpone what you already know you should do, that is to repent and believe the Gospel, to believe into Jesus Christ, in order to be Saved. If you are counting on being last minute and thinking that you can continue in your sin...take heed!

"And he said to me, Do not seal the Words of the Prophecy of this Book, for the time is at hand. He who is unjust, let him be unjust still; he who is filthy, let him be filthy still; he who is righteous, let him be righteous still; he who is holy, let him be holy still. And behold, I am coming quickly, and My reward is with Me, to give to every one according to what his work shall be." Revelation 22:10-12

"Therefore you also be ready, for the Son of Man comes at an hour you do not expect. Who then is a faithful and wise servant, whom his master made administrator over his household, to give them food in due season? Blessed is that servant whom his master, when he comes, will find so doing. Truly, I say to you that he will appoint him as administrator over all his possessions. But if that wicked servant says in his heart, My master delays his coming, and begins to beat his fellow servants, and to eat and drink with the drunkards, the master of that servant will come on a day when he is not expecting him and in an hour he does not know, and will cut him in two and appoint him his portion with the hypocrites. There shall be weeping and gnashing of teeth." Matthew 24:44-51

So, in essence, perhaps this is the most telling of all of the characteristics of the Antichrist rising to power, his relationship with Israel. While the Bible doesn't say that the Antichrist is Jewish, certainly it would seem to be more believable. Is it possible that the religious Jews and the leaders of Israel would be deceived that the false Messiah, the Antichrist, is a Gentile?

This doesn't seem plausible, yet if the Bible is nearly silent or silent on the race of the Antichrist, then certainly it can't be said that it isn't possible. I also consider how anti-Semitic people are around the globe. The United States, particularly the republican party is certainly pro-Israel, yet the same can not be said with the Middle East, Europe, etc., where anti-Semitism has been on the rise for quite some time.

So I question how a Jewish man could rise to the power of the Antichrist, when he would automatically be hated and called part of a conspiracy by much of the world. I also question how Israel could accept this person as their Messiah, if his heritage was not of Jewish decent.

While this topic is just covering the facts here and also a few theories, in regards to Bible prophecy, I can not help but to mention President Trump. The evidence I have seen and have printed out is overwhelming that he is the first Jewish President of the United States. Yet he is not known as a Jew to most of the world.

In Israel, many prominent rabbis believe that he is of the house of David and of Jewish lineage. Their thoughts are that the Messiah is simply a political leader who restores Israel to their rightful place. Should it not be stated that President Trump is trying to make the ultimate peace deal with Israel? Should it not be of interest that President Trump is highly likely Jewish, yet the world does not know that? With the exception of Israel, the only country that it truly would matter, because the Tribulation *("time of Jacob's trouble" Jer. 30:7)* is focused around the restoration of Israel, though the whole world is under God's wrath.

With Jerusalem recognized as the rightful Capital of Israel, with Trump station, now Trump Heights (a new housing division) and a coin featuring Donald Trump from the Temple Mount, the groundwork is obvious laid for a possible large deception. I can not help but to note how President Trump could appease both Israel and the world. While this chapter is not about President Trump, this section must include at least a reference, due to the Jewish reception of him and the references being made by the rabbis that he might be their Messiah.

The other thing that should be mentioned is to tell readers to read Psalms 83. Now does such a scenario where Israel's neighbors attack happen before or after the beginning of the Tribulation? Both would be possible, but with recent news of Israel preparing to attack Iran, etc., that issue should be considered as well. How much better and easier to get a peace deal than after a major war, even if it is brief!

All of this will happen in God's timing, not man's. There has been others who have wanted lasting peace for Israel and numerous peace proposals and even peace treaties that did not last. One thing for certain, as God is in control of the timing of all of these events, is that it will never happen until He allows it to happen. It will not happen until the fullness of the Gentiles is completed *(Ro. 11:25)*. Perhaps this is why there are so many recent problems with forming a government in Israel???

"I was contemplating the horns. And behold, another little horn came up among them, and three of the first horns were uprooted before it. And behold, in this horn were eyes like the eyes of a man, and a mouth speaking great things." Daniel 7:8

"And the ten horns out of this kingdom are ten kings; they shall rise, and another shall rise after them. And he shall be different from the first, and he shall abase three kings." Daniel 7:24

"Then I stood on the sand of the sea. And I saw a beast rising up out of the sea, having seven heads and ten horns, and on his horns ten crowns, and on his heads names of blasphemy." Revelation 13:1

"The ten horns which you saw are ten kings who have received no kingdom as yet, but they receive authority for one hour as kings with the beast." Revelation 17:12

The Antichrist is going to overthrow other kings. When the European Union (EU) was being formed, there were a lot of people who speculated that this was the revived Roman Empire. Originally the EU had ten nations involved in it and they even had currency with a woman riding the beast *(Rev. 17:3)*. I heard these things when I was younger and found them interesting, but when the EU had an 11th nation join them, suddenly it did not seem as interesting. Now the EU has 28 nations that have joined.

What is not well known is the fact that the world can be broken into ten different regions. From what I have heard, originally the Club of Rome were going to call it ten different kingdoms, but then changed the name to regions instead. While this can not be verified, it would fit with biblical prophecy. As times change, the regional powers can change. For instance in the United States we are part of the North American Region (Canada, United States and Mexico).

The Antichrist is going to rule over the revived Roman Empire, which is prophesized in the Bible.

"And the fourth kingdom shall be as *strong as iron. Inasmuch as iron breaks in pieces and shatters all things, and like iron that crushes all these, it will break in pieces and crush. And whereas you saw the feet and the toes, partly of potters' clay and partly of iron,* the *kingdom shall be divided. But there shall be in it the strength of iron, just as you saw the iron mixed with miry clay. And* as *the toes of the feet* were *partly of iron and partly of clay,* so *the kingdom shall be partly strong and partly broken. And as you saw the iron mixed with the miry clay, they shall become mixed with the seed of men. But they shall not cleave to one another, even as iron does not fellowship with clay. And in the days of these kings, the God of Heaven shall set up a kingdom which shall never be destroyed. And the kingdom shall not be left to other people. It shall break in pieces and bring all these kingdoms to an end, and it shall stand forever." Daniel 2:40-44*

"In the first year of Belshazzar, king of Babylon, Daniel saw a dream and visions of his head on his bed. Then he wrote down the dream, telling the main points. Daniel spoke and said, In my vision by night I was looking. And, behold, the four winds of the heavens were stirring up the Great Sea. And four great beasts came up from the sea, different from one another. The first was like a lion and had eagle's wings. I watched until its wings were plucked off. And it was lifted up from the earth and made to stand on two feet like a man, and a man's heart was given to it. And, behold, another beast, a second, like a bear. And it was raised up on one side, and three ribs were *in its mouth between its teeth. And they said this to it, Rise up, devour much flesh. After this I was looking, and, behold, another like a leopard, and it had four wings of a bird on its back. And also the*

beast had four heads. And dominion was given to it. And after this I was looking in the night visions. And, behold, the fourth beast was *frightening and terrifying, and very strong! And it had great iron teeth. It devoured, and broke in pieces, and stamped what was left with its feet. And it was different from all the beasts before it; and it had ten horns. I was contemplating the horns. And behold, another little horn came up among them, and three of the first horns were uprooted before it. And behold, in this horn were eyes like the eyes of a man, and a mouth speaking great things. I watched until the thrones were cast down, and the Ancient of Days sat, whose robe was white as snow and the hair of His head like pure wool. His throne was like flames of fire, its wheels like burning fire. A stream of fire went out and came out from before Him. A thousand thousands served Him, and a vast innumerable number stood before Him. The judgment was set and the books were opened. Then I was watching because of the voice of the great words which the horn spoke. I was watching until the beast was killed, and his body was destroyed and given to the burning flame. As for the rest of the beasts, their dominion was taken away. Yet their lives were prolonged for a season and a time. I saw in the night visions. And behold, one like the Son of Man came with the clouds of the heavens. And He came to the Ancient of Days. And they brought Him near before Him. And dominion was given to Him, and glory, and a kingdom, that all peoples, nations, and languages should serve Him. His dominion is an everlasting dominion which shall not pass away, and His kingdom that which shall not be destroyed. I, Daniel, was distressed in my spirit within my body, and the visions of my head troubled me. And I came near one of those who stood by and asked him the truth of all this. So he told me and made me know the interpretation of the things. These great beasts which are four, are four kings which shall rise up out of the earth. But the saints of the Most High shall receive the kingdom and possess the kingdom forever, even forever and ever. Then I wanted to know the truth of the fourth beast, which was different from all of the others, very frightening, with its teeth of iron and its nails of bronze; which devoured and broke in pieces, and trampled what was left with its feet, also of the ten horns that were on its head, and the other which came up, and before whom three fell, even that horn that had eyes, and a mouth speaking great things, whose appearance was greater than his fellows. I was watching, and the same horn made war with the saints and prevailed against them, until the Ancient of Days came. And judgment was given to the saints of the Most High, and the time came that the saints possessed the kingdom. And he said, The fourth beast shall be the fourth kingdom on earth, which shall be different from all other kingdoms, and shall devour the whole earth, and shall trample it down and break it in pieces. And the ten horns out of this kingdom are ten kings; they shall rise, and another shall rise after them. And he shall be different from the first, and he shall abase three kings. And he shall speak words against the Most High, and shall continually harass the saints of the Most High. And he shall intend to change times and law. And they shall be given into his hand for a period of a time and times and one half time. But the court shall sit, and they shall take away his dominion, to consume and to destroy until the end. And the kingdom and dominion, and the greatness of the kingdoms under the whole heavens shall be given to the people of the saints of the Most High, whose kingdom is an everlasting kingdom. And all dominions shall serve and obey Him. Thus far is the end of the matter. As for me, Daniel, my thoughts terrified me much, and my countenance changed in me. But I kept the matter in my heart." Daniel 7

So there are these theories that are commonly held, or I guess they are not commonly held nowadays and no one is really talking about them. But one of the theories or assumptions is that the Antichrist just simply starts off ruling over all of the world and there is no other 'kings' contesting him. Well quite clearly the Antichrist destroys three of these kings.

Put in another way, the rise of the Antichrist is not going to be without other nations contesting him, or else why would there be war or rumors of war. Who has to fight a battle when you can win without a shot fired? Already the world is on edge with battles of words, yet so far it hasn't turned into an actual war. This has been going on for quite a few years, take our relationship with Russia, it hasn't been good for quite some time.

The point here is, the Antichrist's rise to power will include a miracle of his deadly wound being healed, confirming a peace treaty involving Israel, as well as the overthrow of other kings. The exact timing of these events in relation to the Rapture is not made known. Most people assume that the starting gun is the peace deal with Israel, but could there be a short space of time after the Rapture until then??? Also remember, would not that deal be made behind closed doors before it was publicly known? Personally, if you have heard the Gospel and believed it, but refuse to repent, I would advise you to reconsider your stance, while you still can.

"For He says: In an acceptable time I have heard you, and in a day of salvation I have helped you. Behold, now is the accepted time; behold, now is the day of salvation." 2nd Corinthians 6:2

Other Prophecies Regarding the Antichrist

"Know, therefore, and understand that from the going forth of the word to restore and to rebuild Jerusalem, to Messiah the Prince, shall be seven weeks and sixty two weeks. The street shall be built again, and the wall, even in times of distress. And after sixty two weeks, Messiah shall be cut off, but not for Himself. And the people of a coming ruler shall destroy the city and the sanctuary. And its end shall be with a flood, and desolations are determined, and there shall be war until the end. And he shall confirm a covenant with many for one week. And in the middle of the week he shall cause the sacrifice and the grain offering to cease. And on a corner will be abominations that cause horror, even until the end. And that which was decreed shall be poured out on the desolate." Daniel 9:25-27

"Now brethren, concerning the coming of our Lord Jesus Christ, and of our gathering together to Him, we ask you not to be quickly disturbed in mind or alarmed, either by spirit or by word or by letter, as if from us, as though the Day of Christ has come. Let no one deceive you by any means; for that Day will not come unless the falling away comes first, and the man of sin is unveiled, the son of perdition, who opposes and exalts himself above all that is called God or that is honored, so that he sits as God in the temple of God, declaring of himself that he is God. Do you not remember that when I was still with

20

you I told you these things? And now you know what is restraining, that he may be unveiled in his own time. For the mystery of lawlessness is already at work; only He is now restraining, until it is raised from out of the midst. And then the lawless one will be unveiled, whom the Lord will consume with the breath of His mouth and destroy with the brightness of His coming. The coming of the lawless one is according to the working of Satan, with all power, signs, and lying wonders, and with all unrighteous deception among those who are perishing, because they did not receive the love of the truth, that they might be saved. And for this reason God will send them strong delusion, that they should believe the lie, that they all may be judged who did not believe the truth but had pleasure in unrighteousness." 2nd Thessalonians 2:1-12

"Little children, it is the last hour; and as you have heard that the Antichrist is coming, even now many antichrists have risen up, by which we know that it is the last hour." 1st John 2:18

"Then I stood on the sand of the sea. And I saw a beast rising up out of the sea, having seven heads and ten horns, and on his horns ten crowns, and on his heads names of blasphemy. And the beast which I saw was like a leopard, his feet were like the feet of a bear, and his mouth like the mouth of a lion. And the dragon gave him his power, his throne, and great authority. And I saw one of his heads as if it had been mortally wounded, and his deadly wound was healed. And all the world marveled at the beast. So they did homage to the dragon who gave authority to the beast; and they did homage to the beast, saying, Who is like the beast? Who is able to make war with him? And he was given a mouth speaking great things and blasphemies, and he was given authority to continue for forty-two months. And he opened his mouth in blasphemy against God, to blaspheme His name, His tabernacle, and those who dwell in Heaven. And it was granted to him to make war with the saints and to overcome them. And authority was given him over every tribe, tongue, and nation. And all who dwell on the earth will do homage to him, whose names have not been written in the Book of Life of the Lamb slain from the foundation of the world. If anyone has an ear, let him hear. He who leads into captivity shall go into captivity; he who kills with the sword must be killed with the sword. Here is the endurance and the faith of the saints. Then I saw another beast coming up out of the earth, and he had two horns like a lamb and spoke like a dragon. And he exercises all the authority of the first beast in his presence, and causes the earth and those who dwell in it to do homage to the first beast, whose deadly wound was healed. And he performs great signs, so that he even makes fire come down from heaven onto the earth in the sight of men. And he leads astray those who dwell on the earth by means of those signs which he was granted to do in the presence of the beast, telling those who dwell on the earth to make an image to the beast who was wounded by the sword and lived. And it was given to him to give spirit to the image of the beast, that the image of the beast should both speak and cause as many as would not do homage to the image of the beast to be killed. And he causes all, both small and great, rich and poor, free and slave, to receive a mark on their right hand or on their foreheads, so that no one may buy or sell except one who has the mark or the name of the beast, or the number of his name. Here is wisdom. Let him who has understanding calculate the number of the beast, for it is the number of a man, and his number is 666." Revelation 13

Timeframe of the Rule of the Antichrist

"And he shall confirm a covenant with many for one week. And in the middle of the week he shall cause the sacrifice and the grain offering to cease. And on a corner will be abominations that cause horror, even until the end. And that which was decreed shall be poured out on the desolate." Daniel 9:27

"And he was given a mouth speaking great things and blasphemies, and he was given authority to continue for forty-two months." Revelation 13:5

"And I heard the man clothed in linen, who was on the waters of the river, when he held up his right and his left hand to the heavens and swore by Him who lives forever, that it shall be for a time, times, and a half. And when they have made an end of scattering the power of the holy people, all these things shall be finished. And I heard, but I did not understand. And I said, O my lord, what shall be the end of these things? And He said, Go your way, Daniel! For the words are closed up and sealed until the time of the end. Many shall be purified and made white and tested, but the wicked shall do wickedly. And none of the wicked shall understand, but the wise shall understand. And from the time the regular sacrifice shall be taken away, and the abomination that causes horror is set up, there shall be one thousand, two hundred and ninety days. Blessed is he who waits and comes to the thousand, three hundred and thirty five days. But you, go on to the end, for you shall rest and stand for your inheritance at the end of the days." Daniel 12:7-13

The assumption, and it may very well be, is that the Antichrist will have full power and rule the world for 7 full years. The Tribulation will last 7 years, though there are an interesting few extra days that are mentioned in Daniel that could have to do with Matthew 24:29??? However, during the last 3 1/2 years, total power seems to be had by the Antichrist. Could it be that the Antichrist will not have -total- power until the middle of the week (7 years)?

Then the abomination of desolation is setup. This seems to correspond with these verses:

"Therefore when you see the abomination of desolation, spoken of by Daniel the prophet, standing in the holy place (whoever reads, let him understand), then let those who are in Judea flee into the mountains." Matthew 24:15-16

"Then the woman fled into the wilderness, where she has a place prepared by God, that they should feed her there one thousand two hundred and sixty days." Revelation 12:6

"And he was given a mouth speaking great things and blasphemies, and he was given authority to continue for forty-two months." Revelation 13:5

There is much about the Antichrist and the Tribulation that simply can not be known. Literally it will make sense when it happens and one can only ponder some of these hings, but can not ascertain as to exactly what will take place or what could possibly fulfill such prophecies.

"But you, O Daniel, shut up the words and seal the book, to the time of the end. Many shall run to and fro, and knowledge shall be increased." Daniel 12:4

"And He said, Go your way, Daniel! For the words are closed up and sealed until the time of the end." Daniel 12:9

Essentially the Antichrist will tread the Holy Land for 42 months or 3 1/2 years, this being the second half of the Tribulation.

"But leave out the court which is outside the temple, and do not measure it, for it has been given to the Gentiles. And they will tread the holy city underfoot for forty-two months." Revelation 11:2

The Antichrist will Rule the Entire World and the Economy

"And he said, The fourth beast shall be the fourth kingdom on earth, which shall be different from all other kingdoms, and shall devour the whole earth, and shall trample it down and break it in pieces." Daniel 7:23

"And it was granted to him to make war with the saints and to overcome them. And authority was given him over every tribe, tongue, and nation." Revelation 13:7

"And he leads astray those who dwell on the earth by means of those signs which he was granted to do in the presence of the beast, telling those who dwell on the earth to make an image to the beast who was wounded by the sword and lived. And it was given to him to give spirit to the image of the beast, that the image of the beast should both speak and cause as many as would not do homage to the image of the beast to be killed. And he causes all, both small and great, rich and poor, free and slave, to receive a mark on their right hand or on their foreheads, so that no one may buy or sell except one who has the mark or the name of the beast, or the number of his name. Here is wisdom. Let him who has understanding calculate the number of the beast, for it is the number of a man, and his number is 666." Revelation 13:14-18

Will the Antichrist rule over the entire world immediately for 7 years or for 3 1/2 years??? Nonetheless, the Antichrist will have risen to power, even though full power might not be there until the second half, he will still be in control. After all, if three kings are abased, there will be some sort of war, whether it involves the military or sheer threat of force.

You often hear the terms one world currency or one world government. Yet the Bible is clear that there will still be nations, though the Antichrist will rule over all of them.

"When the Son of Man comes in His glory, and all the holy angels with Him, then He will sit on the throne of His glory. And all the nations will be gathered before Him, and He

will separate them one from another, as a shepherd divides the sheep from the goats."
Matthew 25:31-32

The Antichrist will have total control over the world economy.

"And he causes all, both small and great, rich and poor, free and slave, to receive a mark on their right hand or on their foreheads, so that no one may buy or sell except one who has the mark or the name of the beast, or the number of his name." Revelation 13:16-17

For years there have been talk of a one world currency and people have been looking to such. A single worldwide currency might very well fit into the prophecy from Revelation. Clearly the Antichrist has total control over all financial aspects of the world economy. Whether you live in Peru, the United States, China or the Democratic Republic of Congo, you can be assured that no one will be allowed to buy or sell without the mark of the beast.

In order to be able to have such a system in place, there must also be a system of control over the world economy. Perhaps to the folly of the masses (if there is even masses who believe such a thing anymore), the idea of a single currency for all nations may not be reality. With the arrival of bitcoins and other digital currency, there are some speculating that this will be the a one world currency. Perhaps, as cash in hand could still seemingly buy things on the black market around the world.

However, in the times we live there is a financial bubble around the world that is of extraordinary quantity. Recently someone stated the following in a financial article:

"The U.S. economy is a house of cards, built on quicksand, with a tsunami on the way." -
Doug Casey, InternationalMan.com

This isn't just the United States, but the same problems are seen throughout the entire world. Anywhere where there is some wealth, there is also a bubble, in most cases of proportions larger than ever seen before...and the investing into this 'great' economy just doesn't stop. The stage appears to be set to allow for a controlled currency to come into play across the world. When the economy pops, and that will be when the global financial elite want it to, then it seems highly probable that the US dollar will lose it's reserve currency status.

Hidden behind the scenes, yet also in the public domain, there has been Special Drawing Rights (SDR) units for years. Essentially it is a one world currency, but instead of being a single currency, it uses a basket of currencies around the world to replace a single nation from holding the reserve currency of the world.

Take into consideration also that the International Monetary Fund (IMF) has been openly discussing a global reset. The amount of debt around the world held by corporations, governments and individuals is so much that it is NOT possible for it to all be paid back. The solution could simply be that all of the debt is forgiven and perhaps the reserve currency is changed, switching into a new type of currency, though one might very well still use their currencies of their respective nations.

This scenario or similar ones certainly seem ripe to the possibly that the man of the hour, the Antichrist, might be the one who would seemingly provide the solution to the world's financial woes. After all, allowing the disastrous circumstances of a worldwide depression to begin, people would be scrambling towards a leader who would stop the issue immediately, so that they might once again continue on with normalcy in their lives. Such a leader would certainly be hailed as a hero, as people seem to prefer, both in the government and in their personal lives, to kick the can down the road. Imagine no consequences for such a spectacle as the amount of debt that our world has found ourselves in. Where we should be wholeheartedly following Jesus Christ, serving our Creator, we instead have largely found ourselves serving materialism and the consequences of not being content, nor forcing our governments to be content. These ideas are going to come home to roost one day.

I remember years ago pondering the technology behind such things. Just how would that work, what could be the technology that would allow such things to actual become reality? I wondered how the mark of the beast could work or the worship of the image of the beast. While I certainly don't expect to have all of the answers, nor should anyone and I wouldn't be surprised if everyone where wrong at their guesses. One thing I do know is that things have changed.

I recall that there was a group who was manufacturing rugged basic laptop computers for Africa, in the price range of about $100, a long time ago. Back then there were still many areas of the world that were 'in the dark' with the latest technology. However, I can tell you first hand, after traveling through numerous countries in Central America, that a credit card can now be used just about anywhere.

Even a small hole in the wall shop in a foreign country in Central America is likely to allow the use of a credit card. What I never would have guessed is that smartphones would have come out. Essentially now, there is a computer in the hands of over 42% of adults in the entire world, over 81% of Americans and it is growing at an exponential rate. Just a few years ago, only 35% of Americans had a smart phone, now 96% at least have a cell phone.

This technology could easily allow authentication of a mark of the beast scenario. A lot of people, both in Europe and in major cities in the United States, use their phone as their wallet. One thing that must be remembered is the resistance of the people of the United States.

While I was living in Panama, I was shocked to see that both at banks and regular grocery stores, the workers would login to their computers or cash registers using their thumb print, it was quite common. The United States originally had a healthy resistance of technology, due to the work of fundamental preachers across the United States who had warned that in the future there would be the mark of the beast. Plus with movies like *Left*

Behind, there was a culture of resistance in this country. That culture of resistance is quickly disappearing as the use of such technology slowly erodes away the warnings that were placed with generations of Americans.

Across most of the world, there are many Roman Catholics who are not taught such things by the Catholic church. Most of Central America, South America and Europe are Catholic. Much of Africa is either still dark or Muslim, same as much of the Middle East. Even in Israel, they do not believe the New Testament, so despite the fact of their being some warnings in the Old Testament, they are largely ignorant of such a coming time, thus providing proof of them accepting the false messiah. America was always the part of the world who heard about such things, the resistance should have been expected.

As the apostasy is in full bloom, it is not surprising that Americans no longer have much resistance and though there is still talk of such things, largely their discussions are not based on the Bible, but more of seeking proof for the Bible. They don't believe, but find it interesting.

Why speculate what the mark of the beast might be? There are invisible tattoos, there are very small microchips, though the Bible clearly states that it will be ON the right hand or forehead. That is enough said. Technology clearly exists in the world today that would allow for such a system to be QUICKLY put into place. I would not be surprised if such things were ready to be rolled out upon the world at a frightening pace.

Please do note, the Bible never says that the mark of the beast will be fully going for the entire 7 years of the Tribulation. Perhaps it is just a smaller time period towards the end of that time??? So do not listen to the naysayers who will likely tell people not to worry about a new currency (like the SDR unit) or a new gold backed currency, as there is no mark of the beast associated with it. One can be assured that whatever type of currency is used there will be a mark of the beast EVENTUALLY, for the Bible says so.

A special note about the mark of the beast.

Please note that it is impossible to take the mark of the beast and go to Heaven. Salvation is NOT possible for those who take the mark of the beast (or worship the image of the beast). There MUST be a choice made to either serve God or to serve the Antichrist. For those who were Left Behind, they will ultimately be forced to make such decisions, if they survive long enough during the *("time of Jacob's trouble" Jer. 30:7)*.

"And a third angel followed them, saying with a loud voice, If anyone does homage to the beast and his image, and receives his mark on his forehead or on his hand, he himself shall also drink of the wine of the wrath of God, which is poured out full strength into the cup of His anger. He shall be tormented with fire and brimstone before the holy angels and before the Lamb." Revelation 14:9-10

"And I saw thrones, and they sat on them, and judgment was committed to them; and I saw the souls of those who had been beheaded for their witness to Jesus and for the Word

of God, <u>who had not done homage to the beast or his image, and had not received his</u> *<u>mark on their foreheads or on their hands.</u> And they lived and reigned with Christ for a thousand years." Revelation 20:4*

Antichrist Rules by Miracles & Deception

"The coming of the lawless one is according to the working of Satan, with all power, signs, and lying wonders, and with all unrighteous deception among those who are perishing, because they did not receive the love of the truth, that they might be saved." 2nd Thessalonians 2:9-10

"Then I saw another beast coming up out of the earth, and he had two horns like a lamb and spoke like a dragon. And he exercises all the authority of the first beast in his presence, and causes the earth and those who dwell in it to do homage to the first beast, whose deadly wound was healed. And he performs great signs, so that he even makes fire come down from heaven onto the earth in the sight of men. And he leads astray those who dwell on the earth by means of those signs which he was granted to do in the presence of the beast, telling those who dwell on the earth to make an image to the beast who was wounded by the sword and lived. And it was given to him to give spirit to the image of the beast, that the image of the beast should both speak and cause as many as would not do homage to the image of the beast to be killed." Revelation 13:11-15

Who knows what all of the signs and lying wonders will be? What is known, is that these things will be done through satanic power.

"Then if anyone says to you, Look, here is the Christ; or, There; do not believe it. For false christs and false prophets will arise and show great signs and wonders to lead astray, if possible, even the elect. Behold, I have told you beforehand. Therefore if they say to you, Behold, He is in the desert, do not go out; or, Behold, He is in the inner rooms, do not believe it. For as the lightning comes out of the east and flashes to the west, so also will the coming of the Son of Man be. For wherever the carcass is, there the eagles will be gathered together." Matthew 24:23-28

Take Jesus's words regarding such signs and wonders. Those signs and wonders are to lead astray. Jesus has warned beforehand, take it seriously.

If all of these signs and wonders where evil, would people not automatically declare that this was indeed the Antichrist? Well, Jesus clearly states that if possible, even the elect (Israel) would be lead astray. So likely and logically many of these signs and wonders will be things that would make people consider that the Antichrist, who is doing them, might in fact be the Messiah (or the Christ). Jesus CLEARLY warns not to believe it.

There is no being led astray if someone (rightfully at that time) assumes that these signs and wonders done by the Antichrist are satanic...they will be! At that point and at that time, for anyone who might read this, please just be faithful to Jesus Christ. For those who have truly become born-again at that time, just hold on, until you can't hold on anymore, than you will be at Home with the Lord. Not much else can be said. The deceiver, the Antichrist, will present a very good argument towards himself with these signs and wonders...DO NOT BELIEVE IT!

Homage to the Image of the Beast

"And it was given to him to give spirit to the image of the beast, that the image of the beast should both speak and cause as many as would not do homage to the image of the beast to be killed." Revelation 13:5

The same warnings about not taking the mark of the beast apply to not doing homage to the image of the beast. Do not be deceived, reread that section.

I've often wondered exactly how this would work. However, with smartphones everywhere, now I can imagine a possibility for somehow that technology being used to ensure that the Antichrist has compliance from all citizens. This is serious stuff!

What the image of the beast will be, I do not know. However, the Bible says that this image will both speak AND cause as many as would not do homage to the image of the beast to be killed! Will it report you to the authorities for not doing homage to it? Is that how one will be killed???

The simple fact that the image of the beast speaks is beyond marveling. For in the past God had spoken of such idols that mankind has made in the following ways:

"Every man is stupid in his knowledge; every refiner is dried up by the graven image; for his molten image is a lie, and no breath is in them." Jeremiah 10:14

"Their idols are silver and gold, the work of men's hands. They have mouths, but they do not speak; eyes they have, but they do not see; they have ears, but they do not hear; noses they have, but they do not smell; they have hands, but they do not handle; feet they have, but they do not walk; nor do they utter through their throat. Those who make them are like them; so is everyone who trusts in them." Psalms 115:4-8

I've heard of holographic images that some people have stated will be used to deceive people during the Tribulation, sort of like a Project Blue Beam scenario (don't google it if you are living during that time...dangerous to do so), essentially a government plot to deceive the masses, something of the order that might be used to explain away the Rapture with a fake alien invasion or other worldly 'aliens', yet done with deception of high technology. Yet the Bible says here that the image of the beast speaks.

Simply put, this is likely just another lying wonder that is satanic in nature and allowed to happen. What will the image of the beast be? If the Bible isn't more specific than that, how can I be? I've thought about such things before and think of some of the technology that we have, like robots, but a robot just wouldn't make sense.

Already there are robots who talk (speak) through computer programming. Such a thing wouldn't really be that out of the ordinary for most people in this day and age, so I assume it is probably something much more than that. Whatever it is, certainly the breath' that is given to it (allowing it to speak) will be supernatural.

"And all who dwell on the earth will do homage to him, whose names have not been written in the Book of Life of the Lamb slain from the foundation of the world." Revelation 13:8

God has known those who would choose to follow Him, through His Son Jesus Christ. Yes, plan on being killed for not worshipping the beast, however, for those who have truly repented and believed into Jesus Christ as their Lord and Savior, whose names are written in the Book of Life, note that Jesus will certainly be waiting to receive you.

The Antichrist is a Blasphemer and a Murderer

"So they did homage to the dragon who gave authority to the beast; and they did homage to the beast, saying, Who is like the beast? Who is able to make war with him? And he was given a mouth speaking great things and blasphemies, and he was given authority to continue for forty-two months. And he opened his mouth in blasphemy against God, to blaspheme His name, His tabernacle, and those who dwell in Heaven. And it was granted to him to make war with the saints and to overcome them. And authority was given him over every tribe, tongue, and nation." Revelation 13:4-7

"You are of the devil as your father, and the lusts of your father you purpose to do. He was a murderer from the beginning, and does not stand in the truth, because there is no truth in him. When he speaks a lie, he speaks from his own, for he is a liar and the father of it." John 8:44

Jesus said:

"And I also say to you that you are Peter, and on this Rock I will build My church, and the gates of Hades shall not prevail against It." Matthew 16:18

Also from 2nd Thessalonians:

"For the mystery of lawlessness is already at work; only He is now restraining, until it is raised from out of the midst." 2nd Thessalonians 2:7

So the Antichrist will declare himself to be God.

...*"who opposes and exalts himself above all that is called God or that is honored, so that he sits as God in the temple of God, declaring of himself that he is God."* 2nd Thessalonians 2:4

One who declares to be God is as blasphemous as it can get. Yet the Antichrist will be doing so for 3 1/2 years, speaking great things and blaspheming! Also the Antichrist will be given power to rule all of the world, but also to overcome the saints.

So for those who hear of such things after the Tribulation has already begun, please understand that the Antichrist is going to be allowed to make all of the saints martyrs. For the Bible also speaks of these martyrs:

"And when He opened the fifth seal, I saw under the altar the souls of those who had been slain because of the Word of God and because of the testimony which they held. And they cried with a loud voice, saying, How long, O Lord, holy and true, until You judge and avenge our blood on those who dwell on the earth? And a white robe was given to each one of them; and it was said to them that they should rest a little while longer, until both the number of their fellow servants and their brethren, who were about to be killed as they were, was filled up." Revelation 6:9-11

"After these things I looked, and behold, a great multitude which no one was able to number, of all nations, tribes, peoples, and tongues, standing before the throne and before the Lamb, clothed with white robes, with palm branches in their hands, and crying out with a loud voice, saying, Salvation belongs to our God who sits on the throne, and to the Lamb! And all the angels stood around the throne and the elders and the four living creatures, and fell on their faces before the throne and did homage to God, saying: Amen. Blessing and glory and wisdom, thanksgiving and honor and power and might, be to our God forever and ever. Amen. Then one of the elders answered, saying to me, Who are these arrayed in white robes, and where did they come from? And I said to him, Sir, you know. So he said to me, These are the ones coming out of great affliction, and have washed their robes and made them white in the blood of the Lamb. Therefore they are before the throne of God, and serve Him day and night in His temple. And He who sits on the throne will spread His tabernacle over them. They shall neither hunger anymore nor thirst anymore; the sun shall not fall on them, nor any burning heat; for the Lamb who is in the midst of the throne will shepherd them and lead them to living fountains of waters. And God will wipe away every tear from their eyes." Revelation 7:9-17

So undoubtedly a great multitude, which no one is able to number, will become martyrs during this time. If we consider history and consider what the Roman Catholic church did by killing millions upon millions of professing Christians throughout The Inquisition, yet the Church survived. Under the Antichrist, power is given unto him to overcome the saints.

So why? How can this be? How can it be that God would allow such a thing to take place?

Do you not know the Word of God? Have you not heard? Have you not been taught? Where are the preachers who are warning about these things? Why aren't those who call themselves God's people watching and ready?

When the Rapture happens, the Tribulation begins, the Antichrist rises to power, quite possibly continuing to rise to power. The second the Rapture happens, the Church age is over *(Rev. 4:1)*.

That moment is the darkest moment in all of history. There is not a single man, woman or child on the entire planet who truly knows God, who truly is Saved. Every pastor who is still there, every Bible professing individual, every person who says they are saved, every single person around on the WHOLE planet are not Saved, at that very moment. There is not a single time throughout history that a man (or woman) has not had an ongoing true relationship with their Creator...not one, not from Adam until the point that the Rapture happens.

However, the Church age does not go on forever, the Rapture ends it. For Christ in no uncertain words proclaimed the following:

"He who is unjust, let him be unjust still; he who is filthy, let him be filthy still; he who is righteous, let him be righteous still; he who is holy, let him be holy still. And behold, I am coming quickly, and My reward is with Me, to give to every one according to what his work shall be." Revelation 22:11-12

Harsh stuff, yes it is. For the apostasy, the deception of the false churches throughout the world has been very great. Yet God was not far from anyone, had they truly sought to seek Him.

"And you shall seek Me and find Me, when you search for Me with all your heart." Jeremiah 29:13

The invitation was there and still is. I would imagine that those who are judged and will believe the 'strong delusion' will not have that chance. Those who do homage to the image of the beast or take the mark of the beast (which may go hand in hand) will certainly not have that chance. Yet, if you are seeking God with all your heart, He will be found by you.

During the Tribulation, things are not as simple now. There is no choice, but to become a martyr. There is no choice but to accept Jesus Christ as your Savior, even unto death.

"I was watching, and the same horn made war with the saints and prevailed against them,"... Daniel 7:21

"For this God is our God forever and ever; He will be our guide even unto death." Psalms 48:14

So, this being written for those who were Left Behind, just how did the doctrine of Salvation minus repentance go for you? Just how well was the blasphemous concerts in the supposed houses of God (churches) for society? How well were those preachers, who are still on this earth, that said that God accepted gay marriage and other absolute clearly unbiblical stances?!

This was always serious business because God has always been Holy and He still is!

"Therefore gird up the loins of your mind, be sober, and rest your hope fully upon the grace that is to be brought to you at the revelation of Jesus Christ; as obedient children, not conforming yourselves to the former lusts in your ignorance; but as He who called you is holy, you also become holy in all conduct, because it is written, Be holy, because I am holy." 1st Peter 1:13-16

Well now what? The same thing as should have been preached before, repent and believe into Jesus Christ, who died for your sins on the Cross and be Saved!

..." testifying both to Jews, and also to Greeks, repentance toward God and faith toward our Lord Jesus Christ." Acts 20:21

"For to this you were called, because Christ also suffered for us, leaving us an example, that you should follow His steps: Who committed no sin, nor was deceit found in His mouth; who, when He was reviled, did not revile in return; when He suffered, He did not threaten, but gave Himself over to Him who judges righteously; who Himself bore our sins in His own body on the tree, that we, having died to sins, might live unto righteousness; by whose stripes you were healed. For you were like sheep going astray, but have now returned to the Shepherd and Overseer of your souls." 1st Peter 2:21-25

"For God so loved the world that He gave His only begotten Son, that everyone believing into Him should not perish but have eternal life. For God did not send His Son into the world to judge the world, but that the world through Him might be saved. The one believing into Him is not judged; but the one not believing is judged already, because he has not believed in the name of the only begotten Son of God." John 3:16-18

"But what does it say? The Word is near you, in your mouth and in your heart (that is, the Word of Faith which we preach): that if you confess with your mouth the Lord Jesus and believe in your heart that God has raised Him from the dead, you will be saved. For with the heart one believes unto righteousness, and with the mouth confession is made unto salvation. For the Scripture says, Everyone believing on Him will not be put to shame. For there is no distinction between Jew and Greek, for the same Lord over all is rich toward all who call upon Him. For everyone, whoever calls on the name of the Lord shall be saved." Romans 10:8-13

Call on the name of the Lord and be Saved! Are you going to continue to listen to what others (who were also Left Behind) are saying still?! Do not put your trust in man, put your trust in God. For to those who are reading this during the Tribulation, trust God, just trust Him.

"And it shall come to pass that everyone who shall call on the name of the Lord shall be saved." Acts 2:21

"And it shall be, that whoever shall call on the name of Jehovah shall escape. For in Mount Zion and in Jerusalem shall be deliverance, as Jehovah has said, and among the survivors whom Jehovah shall call." Joel 2:32

For those who are reading this beforehand, you better get busy doing the same or you will be Left Behind, this is serious business, this is no joke.

"For we did not follow cunningly devised fables when we made known to you the power and coming of our Lord Jesus Christ, but were eyewitnesses of His majesty. For He received from God the Father honor and glory when such a voice came to Him from the Excellent Glory: This is My beloved Son, in whom I am well pleased. And we heard this voice which came from Heaven when we were with Him on the holy mountain. And so we also have a more sure Word of prophecy, which you do well to heed as to a light that shines in a dark place, until the day dawns and the morning star rises in your hearts; knowing this first, that not any of the prophecies of Scripture came into being from personal exposition, for prophecy was not formerly brought forth by man's choice, but holy men of God spoke as they were propelled along by the Holy Spirit." 2nd Peter 1:16-21

The Antichrist is a Destroyer

"And he said, The fourth beast shall be the fourth kingdom on earth, which shall be different from all other kingdoms, and shall devour the whole earth, and shall trample it down and break it in pieces." Daniel 7:23

"And his power shall be mighty, but not by his own power. And he shall destroy extraordinarily, and he shall prosper, and work, and destroy the mighty and the holy people." Daniel 8:24

This is the revived Roman Empire that has already been mentioned. Once again the power of the Antichrist is NOT his own power, but the workings of Satan. As mentioned earlier, there is a reason that Israel will flee, for the Antichrist will not just destroy, he will destroy extraordinarily!

Exactly what takes place and how it plays out is not known. Yet God's Word will be true on this, just as it has been with ever other prophecy that has been fulfilled.

"For what if some did not believe? Will their unbelief nullify the faithfulness of God? Let it not be! Indeed, let God be true but every man a liar. As it is written: That You may be found just in Your words, and may win the case when You are judged. But if our unrighteousness demonstrates the righteousness of God, what shall we say? Is God unjust who lays on wrath? (I speak as a man.) Let it not be! Otherwise, how will God judge the world? For if in my lie, the truth of God has abounded to His glory, why am I

also still judged as a sinner? And why not say (as we are slanderously reported and as some affirm that we say), Let us do evil that good may come? Their condemnation is just. What then? Do we surpass them? Not at all. For we have previously charged both Jews and Greeks, that they are all under sin. As it is written: There is none righteous, no, not one; there is none who understands; there is none who seeks after God." Romans 3:3-11

The Antichrist has Great Intelligence and is a Deceiver

"And also through his cunning he will cause deceit to prosper in his hand. And he will magnify himself in his heart, and through prosperity shall destroy many. He shall also stand up against the Ruler of rulers, but he shall be broken in pieces without hands." Daniel 8:25

Not only does the Antichrist understand sinister schemes, but he is cunning and deceit prospers in his hand. The Antichrist will be able to manipulate the masses of people. He will be a man who causes prosperity, which shall destroy many.

All over the world there is a desire for things to be better economically. Now in the United States we actually have a man in office who preaches a prosperity doctrine. Yet, jobs, more jobs and better living has been the argument for many past Presidents and will undoubtedly be the same argument for future leaders all around the world. People want to prosper, yet why not be rich toward God and seek those riches which are found in Christ.

"Then He spoke a parable to them, saying: The ground of a certain rich man yielded plentifully. And he thought within himself, saying, What shall I do, since I have nowhere to gather my fruits? So he said, I will do this: I will pull down my barns and build larger, and there I will gather all my fruits and my goods. And I will say to my soul, Soul, you have many goods laid up for many years; take your ease; eat, drink, and be merry. But God said to him, Fool! This night your soul will be required of you; then whose will those things be which you have prepared? So is he who lays up treasure for himself, and is not rich toward God." Luke 12:16-21

"To me, who am less than the least of all the saints, this grace was given, that I should preach among the Gentiles the unsearchable riches of Christ," Ephesians 3:8

Perhaps the prosperity doctrine will be at a time when people should be searching for God, rather than for their own personal wealth? Perhaps that will be the cause of destruction through prosperity???

In the end the Antichrist will be destroyed by Jesus Christ, who will be returning with the saints.

"And then the lawless one will be unveiled, whom the Lord will consume with the breath of His mouth and destroy with the brightness of His coming." 2nd Thessalonians 2:8

"And I saw Heaven opened, and behold, a white horse. And He who sat on him was called Faithful and True, and in righteousness He judges and makes war. His eyes were like a flame of fire, and on His head were many crowns. He had a name written that no one knew except Himself. And He was clothed with a robe dipped in blood, and His name is called The Word of God. And the armies in Heaven, clothed in fine linen, white and pure, followed Him on white horses. And out of His mouth goes a sharp sword, that with it He might strike the nations. And He Himself will rule them with a rod of iron. He Himself treads the winepress of the fierceness and wrath of Almighty God. And He has on His robe and on His thigh a name written: KING OF KINGS AND LORD OF LORDS. And I saw an angel standing in the sun; and he cried with a loud voice, saying to all the birds that fly in the midst of the heavens, Come and gather together for the supper of the great God, that you may eat the flesh of kings, the flesh of commanders, the flesh of mighty men, the flesh of horses and of those who sit on them, and the flesh of all people, free and slave, both small and great. And I saw the beast, the kings of the earth, and their armies, gathered together to make war against Him who sat on the horse and against His army. And the beast was captured, and with him the false prophet who worked signs in his presence, by which he led astray those who received the mark of the beast and those who did homage to his image. These two were cast alive into the Lake of Fire burning with brimstone. And the rest were killed with the sword which proceeded out of the mouth of Him who sat on the horse. And all the birds were filled with their flesh." Revelation 19:11-21

"Behold, the day of Jehovah comes, and your spoils shall be divided in your midst. For I will gather all the nations to battle against Jerusalem. And the city shall be captured, and the houses plundered, and the women ravished. And half the city shall go into captivity and the rest of the people shall not be cut off from the city. And Jehovah shall go forth and fight against those nations, like the day He fought in the day of battle. And His feet shall stand in that day on the Mount of Olives, which is before Jerusalem on the east; and the Mount of Olives shall split in two, from the east even to the west, a very great valley. And half of the mountain shall move toward the north, and half of it toward the south. And you shall flee to the valley of My mountains, for the valley of the mountains shall reach to Azal. And you shall flee as you fled before the earthquake in the days of Uzziah, king of Judah. And Jehovah my God shall come, and all the saints with You. And it will come to pass in that day, that there shall not be light; the great lights will shrink. And it will be one day which shall be known to Jehovah; not day and not night, but it will happen, that there will be light at evening time. And it shall be in that day, that living waters shall go out from Jerusalem, half of them toward the eastern sea, and half of them toward the western sea; in summer and in winter it shall be. And Jehovah shall be King over all the earth. In that day there shall be one Jehovah, and His name one." Zechariah 14:1-9

"Behold, I will make Jerusalem a cup of trembling to all the peoples all around, and it shall also be against Judah in the siege against Jerusalem. And in that day I will make Jerusalem a heavy stone for all the peoples; all who lift it shall be slashed; cut to pieces. And all the nations of the earth will be gathered against it. In that day I will strike every horse with bewilderment and his rider with madness, says Jehovah. And I will open My *eyes on the house of Judah, and will strike every horse of the people with blindness. And the governors of Judah shall say in their heart, The inhabitants of Jerusalem shall be my strength in Jehovah of Hosts, their God. In that day I will make the governors of Judah like a hearth of fire among the wood, and like a torch of fire among cut grain. And they shall devour all the peoples all around, on the right hand and on the left. And Jerusalem shall be inhabited again in her own place, in Jerusalem. Jehovah also shall save the tents of Judah first, so that the glory of the house of David and the glory of the inhabitants of Jerusalem may not be magnified above Judah. In that day Jehovah shall defend the inhabitants of Jerusalem. And he who is feeble among them in that day shall be like David, and the house of David shall be like God, like the Angel of Jehovah before them. And it shall be in that day, that I will seek to destroy all the nations that come against Jerusalem. And I will pour on the house of David, and on the inhabitants of Jerusalem, the Spirit of grace and supplication. And they shall look on Me whom they have pierced; and they shall mourn for Him, as one mourns for an only son, and they shall be bitter over Him, like the bitterness over the firstborn." Zechariah 12:2-10*

Few Final Characteristics of the Antichrist

"And the king shall do according to his own will. And he shall exalt and magnify himself above every god; he shall even speak extraordinary things against the Mighty God of gods and shall prosper until the indignation is complete. For that which is decreed shall be done. He shall not regard the God of his fathers, nor the desire of women; nor regard any god. For he shall magnify himself above them all. But in his place he shall honor the god of fortresses, and he shall honor a god whom his fathers did not know, with gold and silver and with precious stones, and desirable things." Daniel 11:36-38

a.) The Antichrist does according to his own will.

The Antichrist will do what he wants to do and he will prosper at doing it. He will rise to power and subdue, yes with satanic power. He will deceive and he will prosper at doing that.

b.) Desire of women.

All over the internet, it seems to be a popular teaching that the Antichrist will be gay. Perhaps this could be correct, but I tend not to think so. The desire of women is written in the same sentence as having no regard to the God of his fathers (would this not suggest that he must be Jewish???), nor will he regard any god.

Perhaps the Antichrist just won't like women? However, let me introduce another theory on the desire of women.

To those of you men who are married out there. Just how often do you plan on doing something (buying something, making something, whatever) and it happens that your wife is not very happy about it. Do you listen? Do you change your plans?

If you are out shopping for a house and find one that you like, but your wife hates, do you buy it anyway? What?! Do you expect comfort in living in the same house with your wife as she sleeps on the couch or in a different room because she is not happy with you?

Unfortunately, the reality of it is, women get dressed up in order to attract a man and a man goes on dates with the woman for his own purposes. Is this not what has been portrayed in countless movies and television shows? Could one not see this on a day to day basis in real life?

Yet I would suspect that just as the Antichrist would not have any regard towards God Almighty, nor any pagan god, nor the desire of women, that all would be of the same thing. The Antichrist would not care about what he does, as that passage of scripture starts off that he does according to his will.

So the Antichrist is not going to care what God thinks, he isn't go to care what his wife thinks and he has no regard to any other pagan god or what that culture thinks. He would eat a hamburger in India and not think a thing about it, no regard towards it. Now even a Believer should not have regard towards pagan gods, but the Antichrist simply won't care, he will do what he wants.

Even Samson fell for the desire of women:

"Afterward it happened that he loved a woman in the Valley of Sorek, whose name was Delilah. And the rulers of the Philistines came up to her and said to her, Entice him, and find out where his great strength lies, and by what means we may prevail against him, that we may bind him to afflict him; and each of us will give you eleven hundred pieces of silver. And Delilah said to Samson, Please tell me where your great strength lies, and with what you may be bound to afflict you. And Samson said to her, If they bind me with seven fresh shoots, not yet dried, then I shall become weak, and be like any other man. So the rulers of the Philistines brought up to her seven fresh shoots, not yet dried, and she bound him with them. Now men were lying in wait, staying with her in the room. And she said to him, The Philistines are upon you, Samson! But he broke the shoots as a strand of yarn breaks when it touches fire. So the secret of his strength was not known. Then Delilah said to Samson, Behold, you have mocked me and told me lies. Now, please tell me with what you may be bound. So he said to her, If they bind to tie me with new ropes with which no work has been done, then I shall become weak, and be like any other man. Therefore Delilah took new ropes and bound him with them, and said to him, The Philistines are upon you, Samson! And men were lying in wait, staying in the room. But he broke them off his arms like thread. Delilah said to Samson, Until now you have mocked me and told me lies. Tell me with what you may be bound. And he said to her, If you weave the seven locks of my head into the web of the loom; so she wove it tightly with the batten of the loom, and said to him, The Philistines are upon you, Samson! But he awoke from his sleep, and pulled out the batten and the web from the loom. Then she said to him, How can you say, I love you, when your heart is not with me? You have mocked me these three times, and have not told me where your great strength lies. And it came to pass, when she had pressed upon him daily with her words and urged him, so

that his soul was vexed to death, that he told her all his heart, and said to her, No razor has ever come upon my head, for I have been a Nazirite unto God from my mother's womb. If I am shaven, then my strength will leave me, and I shall become weak, and be like any other man. And when Delilah saw that he had told her all his heart, she sent and summoned the rulers of the Philistines, saying, Come up once more, for he has told me all his heart. So the rulers of the Philistines came up to her and brought the money in their hand. And she made him sleep on her knees, and called for a man and had him shave off the seven locks of his head. And she began to afflict him, and his strength depart from him. And she said, The Philistines are upon you, Samson! So he awoke from his sleep, and thought, I will go out as before, at other times, and shake myself free! But he had not perceived that Jehovah had departed from him. And the Philistines took him and bored out his eyes, and brought him down to Gaza. They bound him with bronze fetters, and he was grinding in the prison house." Judges 16:4-21

The Antichrist wouldn't care what his 'Delilah' says.

c.) The Antichrist shall honor the god of fortresses.

One of the definitions, that seem to fit best in our modern day age of technological warfare is the following:

fortress, n.

Defense; safety; security.

Webster's University Dictionary Unabridged, 1942

From the context of the Bible, in light of modern day warfare, the Antichrist seems to be one who will love military might. He will be one who will take the military seriously and ultimately he will use the military or the threat of military force to achieve his objectives. Perhaps, as my best friend has stated, he could use the lack of military support (mutual aid to other countries if they are attacked) in order to meet his objectives.

One thing for certain, however it may play out, the Antichrist will be a military man and someone who shows honor towards the military, likely he will have that proof with investments into the military, new technology and a strong show of force, whether in actual war or as a deterrent to war.

"And I looked, and behold, a white horse. He who sat on it had a bow; and a crown was given to him, and he went out conquering, indeed in order to conquer." Revelation 6:2

If this verse is talking about the Antichrist, notice he has a bow, but no arrows. Also another verse of interest regarding the Antichrist.

"So they did homage to the dragon who gave authority to the beast; and they did homage to the beast, saying, Who is like the beast? Who is able to make war with him?" Revelation 13:4

However it plays out, the Antichrist seems to have control of a powerful military that is able to destroy his enemies.

d.) The Antichrist Shall Intent to Change Times and Law

"And he shall speak words against the Most High, and shall continually harass the saints of the Most High. And he shall intend to change times and law. And they shall be given into his hand for a period of a time and times and one half time."

Whatever this may be, likely will remained sealed until the end *(Da. 12:4)*. I'm sure there are some theories out there, but like much of the 70th Week, better known as the Tribulation *(Da. 9:24-27)*, there is much mystery.

Conclusion

More could be said, more thoughts could be added, but why? Certainly the Bible is quite clear that the Antichrist will eventually rise to power and he will prosper in his endeavors. He will overcome the saints (those who get Saved during the Tribulation), he will rule the world, he will demand to be worshipped and he will control the economy. In the end he will fail and he will be cast into the Lake of Fire.

Why, o' why would those who are Created in the image of God *(Gen. 1:27)* want to also be cast into the Lake of Fire with the Antichrist? Take heed!

If you are looking for the world to fall of the cliff (economically, warfare or otherwise) before the Tribulation, than take this verse into consideration that things -might- be just as they are now when the starting gun of the Rapture happens.

"For as in the days before the flood, they were eating and drinking, marrying and giving in marriage, until the day that Noah entered into the ark, and did not realize until the flood came and took them all away, so also will the coming of the Son of Man be. Then two will be in the field: one is taken and the other is left. Two will be grinding at the mill: one is taken and the other is left. Watch therefore, for you do not know what hour your Lord comes. But know this, that if the master of the house had known what hour the thief comes, he would have watched and not allowed his house to be dug through. Therefore you also be ready, for the Son of Man comes at an hour you do not expect." Matthew 24:38-44

Amen!

A Grand Delusion?

"For the mystery of lawlessness is already at work; only He is now restraining, until it is raised from out of the midst. And then the lawless one will be unveiled, whom the Lord will consume with the breath of His mouth and destroy with the brightness of His coming. The coming of the lawless one is according to the working of Satan, with all power, signs, and lying wonders, and with all unrighteous deception among those who are perishing, because they did not receive the love of the truth, that they might be saved. And for this reason God will send them strong delusion, that they should believe the lie, that they all may be judged who did not believe the truth but had pleasure in unrighteousness." 2nd Thessalonians 2:7-12

There is much writing that has been done over the years regarding the *"time of Jacob's trouble" (Jer. 30:7)*, known better by many as the Tribulation or the Great Tribulation. In fact the Bible talks about this being a time of great affliction.

"For then there will be great affliction, such as has not been since the beginning of the world until this time, no, nor ever shall be." Matthew 24:21

"And I said to him, Sir, you know. So he said to me, These are the ones coming out of great affliction, and have washed their robes and made them white in the blood of the Lamb." Revelation 7:14

"And at that time, Michael shall stand up, the great ruler who stands for the sons of your people. And there shall be a time of distress, such as has not been since there was a nation until that time. And at that time, your people shall be delivered, everyone that shall be found written in the Book." Daniel 12:1

Many people have made 'maps' and timelines of the book of Revelation, which is rightfully called the Revelation of Jesus Christ *(Rev. 1:1)*. They make timelines of the events from the beginning of the book of Revelation to the end of the book, assuming that these are correct, based upon the judgments, etc., throughout the book. With that, I am not in agreement that things are preciously as people assume. For the book of Revelation is a book of past, present and future.

"Write the things which you have seen, and the things which are, and the things which will take place after these things." Revelation 1:19

So shall everything that could be, will be or otherwise are thought to be, be written out one by one, with the author assuming some sort of special knowledge due to the prophecies written in Revelation? No rather, as the book of Revelation of Jesus Christ points to Him being revealed to Israel *(Zec. 12:10)*, as well as to those who remain, the Second Coming and Christ thereafter ruling *(Rev. 20:3, Zec. 8:3; 14:6)*, why shouldn't the focus be on Christ?

"And His feet shall stand in that day on the Mount of Olives, which is before Jerusalem on the east; and the Mount of Olives shall split in two, from the east even to the west, a very great valley. And half of the mountain shall move toward the north, and half of it toward the south." Zechariah 14:4

I don't have any special knowledge about the book of Revelation, no more than any Believer who would studies the Word of God should, but rather I have a question regarding the sincerity in people who enjoy reading these timelines.

How many people read these timelines just as they would read about aliens, ghosts or anything else in those realms? How many people are interested in the Tribulation or the end-times, are equally interested in things of a demonic nature? While a timeline might prove to be even interesting to a real Believer, the question is what about those who are not Saved?

What exactly would the point be in talking about how the sun will scorch the inhabitants of the earth *(Rev. 16:9)*, how the earth is moved *(Is. 13:13)*, how there will be astronomical upheavals *(Joel 3:15-16)* amongst many other things when in good faith I know that many who would read such things would NEVER make it that far along into the Tribulation. Doing some calculations, based upon the numbers in Revelation, one could come to the conclusion that 90% of humanity are killed by the end of the seven year Tribulation *(Da. 9:27)*, also noting that two-thirds of Israel are killed *(Zec. 13:8-9)*.

Rather what should be stated is a strong warning that people should repent and believe into Jesus Christ as their Lord and Savior BEFORE, rather than as some do who are trying to stockpile for the end times! Please remember, we who are Saved will be with the Lord, we will be Raptured out of here BEFORE the *"time of Jacob's trouble" (Jer. 30:7)*.

"For God did not appoint us to wrath, but to obtain salvation through our Lord Jesus Christ,"... 2nd Thessalonians 5:9

"But I do not want you to be ignorant, brethren, concerning those who are asleep, that you sorrow not as others who have no hope. For if we believe that Jesus died and rose again, even so God will bring with Him those who sleep in Jesus. For this we say to you by the Word of the Lord, that we who are alive and remain until the coming of the Lord will by no means precede those who are asleep. For the Lord Himself will descend from Heaven with a shouted *command, with the voice of the archangel, and with the trumpet of God. And the dead in Christ will rise first. Then we who are alive and remain shall be caught up together* at the same time *with them in the clouds to meet the Lord in the air. And thus we shall always be with the Lord. Therefore encourage one another with these words." 1st Thessalonians 4:13-18*

"<u>After these things</u> I looked, and behold, a door having been opened in Heaven." Revelation 4:1a

So instead of reading in hopes of hearing of fantastic things in the future, rather, consider one's heart before their Creator. For life has been tarrying on in this world for nearly 2,000 years since Jesus went Home *(Ac. 1:9)* to sit at the right hand of the Father *(Mk. 16:19)* Yet, Jesus quite clearly warned, as well as the Holy Scriptures, that eventually the end will come.

"And this gospel of the kingdom will be preached in all the world as a testimony to all the nations, and then the end will come." Matthew 24:14

"And many of those sleeping in the earth's dust shall awake, some to everlasting life, and some to reproach and *everlasting abhorrence." Daniel 12:2*

The question that needs to be asked is whether or not the world is being primed right now for a grand delusion. That question will remain unanswered.

Though evidence will be stated explaining how it seems as though it is possible, the truth of the matter is no one could know until afterwards.

"For the mystery of lawlessness is already at work; only He is now restraining, until it is raised from out of the midst. And then the lawless one will be unveiled, whom the Lord will consume with the breath of His mouth and destroy with the brightness of His coming." 2nd Thessalonians 2:7-8

So why write about such a possibility at all, if it is not possible to know for sure?

Ezekiel was told:

"Son of man, I have made you a watchman for the house of Israel; therefore hear the Word from My mouth, and give them warning from Me: When I say to the wicked, You shall die the death, and you give him no warning, nor speak to warn the wicked from his wicked way, to save his life, that same wicked man shall die in his iniquity; but his blood I will require at your hand. Yet, if you warn the wicked, and he does not turn from his wickedness, nor from his wicked way, he shall die in his iniquity; but you have delivered your soul. Again, when a righteous man turns from his righteousness and commits iniquity, and I lay a stumbling block before him, he shall die. Because you did not give him warning, he shall die in his sin, and his righteousness which he has done shall not be remembered; but his blood I will require at your hand. Nevertheless if you warn the righteous man that the righteous should not sin, and he does not sin, he shall live life because he took warning; and you have delivered your soul." Ezekiel 3:17-21

I heavily considered these things. I thought about the burden on my heart to write such things, I pondered. I scoured the internet looking for what others might be saying. I searched news sources, blogs and numerous web pages, looking for inklings of truth. Was there anyone who pondered that such things could be occurring?; but I came up empty handed each time.

Now perhaps there are some who question the current world events and political situations that not only Americans find themselves in, but also citizens all across the world in there respective nations as well. If perhaps the example that I am using as a backdrop to such an idea whereto in actuality become factual, though I wouldn't know it before the Rapture *(2 Thes. 2:8)*, what could be some of the ramifications of writing such things, especially when being in such a narrow or perhaps empty field of writing?

For if by writing such things there happened to be truth to the ordeal, once again not knowing any special revelation, but simply showing how unprepared the world would be or currently is, especially those who call themselves the church, just what could that entail? For if I write such things and there is a chance of there being truth to them, then could that cause the wrath of man against me?

Nonetheless, what more can I say? If the possibility exists, using the Bible as the textbook of evidence, that the Antichrist world government were rising in front of our very eyes, should I not point it out? Should it not be known, even if no one listens. For certainly, I do not want to have the blood on my hands for not giving a warning regarding the condition of blindness among so-called evangelicals Christians, who are in fact doing EXACTLY the opposite of what I am suggesting here.

First, however, it should be pointed out that the Bible has clearly prophesized that an apostasy would happen. Not only that, but then we must take a look at pondering whether or not part of the 'strong delusion' that is spoke about in the opening Bible verses of this are possibly happening already?

"Now brethren, concerning the coming of our Lord Jesus Christ, and of our gathering together to Him, we ask you not to be quickly disturbed in mind or alarmed, either by spirit or by word or by letter, as if from us, as though the Day of Christ has come. Let no one deceive you by any means; <u>for that Day will not come unless the falling away comes first, and the man of sin is unveiled</u>, the son of perdition, who opposes and exalts himself above all that is called God or that is honored, so that he sits as God in the temple of God, declaring of himself that he is God." 2nd Thessalonians 2:1-4

Now some would read this and suggest that the verse in and of itself would provide evidence that the church would go through the Tribulation. Yet, where is the evidence of this in light of the Bible's clear teaching of a Rapture? For those who have their names written in the Book of Life *(Rev. 20:12)*, those who have repented and by faith believed into Jesus Christ as their Lord and Savior.

Rather understand that the Day is speaking about the actual Second Coming, not the appearing of Jesus Christ at what has been coined the Rapture. For just because these verses clearly stipulate the Antichrist sits as God, does not neglect the fact that the Church will not be here. There are courses of action listed here:

1). Falling Away Happens then...
2). Man of Sin Unveiled (Antichrist)

However, somewhere just BEFORE the man of sin is unveiled the true Church, which is those who are actual repented Believers in Jesus Christ, are Raptured. The falling away has already happened and is continuing.

"For the mystery of lawlessness is already at work; only He is now restraining, until it is raised from out of the midst. And then the lawless one will be unveiled, whom the Lord will consume with the breath of His mouth and destroy with the brightness of His coming." 2nd Thessalonians 2:7-8

"And Jehovah shall go forth and fight against those nations, like the day He fought in the day of battle. And His feet shall stand in that day on the Mount of Olives, which is before Jerusalem on the east; and the Mount of Olives shall split in two, from the east even to the west, a very great valley. And half of the mountain shall move toward the north, and half of it toward the south. And you shall flee to the valley of My mountains, for the valley of the mountains shall reach to Azal. And you shall flee as you fled before the earthquake in the days of Uzziah, king of Judah. <u>And Jehovah my God shall come, and all the saints with You.</u>" Zechariah 14:3-5

Now how can all of the saints be coming with Christ, if we are still here? Beware this false doctrine of the Church going through the Tribulation. Trust me, while there will probably still be lies, for those who have eyes to see, those who are actually Saved will be Raptured prior. One must repent and by faith accept Jesus Christ as their Savior or else you will be Left Behind!

However, some more emphasis must be placed on the apostasy. For, who else, but the apostate church and so-called false christians are going to be the ones deceived? The Bible is quite clear that those 'who did not receive the love of the truth' are the ones who will be deceived. Also the Bible is quite cleared that there will be an innumerable amount of people who are Saved during the *"time of Jacob's trouble" (Jer. 30:7).*

"Now the Spirit expressly says that in latter times some will depart from the faith, being devoted to corrupting spirits and doctrines of demons, speaking lies in hypocrisy, having their own conscience seared, forbidding to marry, and commanding to abstain from foods which God created to be partaken with thanksgiving by those who believe and know the truth." 1st Timothy 4:1-3

"But know this, that in the last days perilous times will come: For men will be lovers of themselves, lovers of money, boasters, proud, blasphemers, disobedient to parents, unthankful, unholy, without natural affection, unyielding, slanderers, without self-control, savage, despisers of good, traitors, headstrong, haughty, lovers of pleasure rather than lovers of God, having a form of godliness but denying its power. And from such people turn away. For of this sort are those who creep into households and make captives of gullible women loaded down with sins, led away by various lusts, always learning, but never able to come to the full *true knowledge of the truth. But as Jannes and Jambres opposed Moses, so do these also oppose the truth: men of corrupt minds, reprobate*

concerning the faith; but they will progress no further, for their folly will be manifest to all, as theirs also was." 2nd Timothy 3:1-9

The apostasy is ripe throughout all of which calls itself Christian. There is a remnant that is left that are true Churches of Jesus Christ (not the Latter Days Saint's style) that are faithful to Jesus Christ. There are still those Churches who preach the Gospel faithfully and also are careful about Salvation, knowing that repentance is also necessary.

Yet around the world there are large false churches and cults that include numerous amounts of people. While there might very well be individuals whose hearts are known by God, as a whole they will certainly be Left Behind. The problem is there are many different types of churches all throughout the United States, in particular, that once preached the truth, to some degree, and now have fully embraced the apostasy, this even in more formerly conservative churches, such as Baptist.

The apostasy isn't just limited to those churches that presume to spread lies about God accepting homosexuals, allowing gay marriage or in some cases even advocating abortion. No rather, the large measure is they are simply unrepentant and preach a Gospel message that is so watered down, that they refuse to preach repentance, despite the words of our Lord and Savior.

"I tell you, no; but unless you repent you will all likewise perish." Luke 13:3

They proclaim the masses who raise a hand during an invitation or simply recite a prayer to be Saved. Many will then discipleship them about how they now are Saved and can never lose that Salvation, preaching what God should speak to the individuals heart *(Phil. 1:6, Jn. 10:28)*, rather than just pointing them to the Holy Scriptures and allowing the Lord to deal with them personally *(Jn. 10:27)*.

They rock out in churches, often with women in skimpy clothing dancing on poles up on stage. They go out and even drink beer in church, or enjoy their Starbucks coffee, rather there to socialize, assuming or hoping for a free ticket to Heaven, simply because they believe. Well let me ask you a question, let me point out something to those who think this way and assume all is well.

"You believe that God is One. You do well. Even the demons believe, and shudder." Jacob (James) 2:19

"Enter by the narrow gate; for wide is the gate and broad is the way that leads to destruction, and there are many entering in through it. Because narrow is the gate and distressing is the way which leads unto life, and there are few who find it. Beware of false prophets, who come to you in sheep's clothing, but inwardly they are ravenous wolves. You will know them from their fruits. Do men gather grapes from thornbushes or figs from thistles? Even so, every good tree produces excellent fruit, but a corrupt tree produces evil fruit. A good tree is not able to produce evil fruit, nor is a corrupt tree able to produce excellent fruit. Every tree that does not produce excellent fruit is cut down

and thrown into the fire. Therefore from their fruits you will know them. Not everyone who says to Me, Lord, Lord, will enter the kingdom of Heaven, but he who does the will of My Father in Heaven. Many will say to Me in that day, Lord, Lord, have we not prophesied in Your name, cast out demons in Your name, and done many works of power in Your name? And then I will declare to them, I never knew you; depart from Me, you who work out lawlessness!" Matthew 7:13-23

So who of these who professed faith in Jesus Christ, didn't believe. Think about it, they prophesied in His name, cast out demons in His name and did many works of power in His name. From any outside perspective, they would have been those who were part of the Saved, they would have been part of the real 'church', they would have been those who were going to Heaven and THEY THOUGHT SO THEMSELVES! I tell you then, what were they lacking?

"And to the angel of the church of the Laodiceans write, These things says the Amen, the Faithful and True Witness, the Beginning of the creation of God: I know your works, that you are neither cold nor hot. I would that you were cold or hot. So then, because you are lukewarm, and neither cold nor hot, <u>I will vomit you out of My mouth.</u> Because you say, I am rich, have become wealthy, and have need of nothing; and do not know that you are wretched and miserable and poor and blind and naked; I counsel you to buy from Me gold refined in the fire, that you may be rich; and white garments, that you may be clothed, that the shame of your nakedness may not be revealed; and anoint your eyes with eye salve, that you may see. As many as I love, I rebuke and chasten. <u>Therefore be zealous and repent.</u> Behold, I stand at the door and knock. If anyone hears My voice and opens the door, I will come in to him and dine with him, and he with Me. To him who overcomes I will grant to sit with Me on My throne, as I also overcame and sat down with My Father on His throne. He who has an ear, let him hear what the Spirit says to the churches." Revelation 3:14-22

Repentance is a necessary component of Salvation and was preached by Jesus and the early apostles, as well as the early Church, even much into the 1950's.

Once again, what were those who were denied entrance into Heaven lacking, if not repentance?

"Now after John was put in prison, Jesus came into Galilee, preaching the gospel of the kingdom of God, and saying, The time is fulfilled, and the kingdom of God is at hand. Repent, and believe in the gospel." Mark 1:14-15

"Then Peter said to them, Repent, and let every one of you be immersed in the name of Jesus Christ to the remission of sins; and you shall receive the gift of the Holy Spirit. For the promise is to you and to your children, and to all who are afar off, as many as the Lord our God will call." Acts 2:38-39

..."testifying both to Jews, and also to Greeks, repentance toward God and faith toward our Lord Jesus Christ." Acts 20:21

"Truly, these times of ignorance God overlooked, but now commands all men everywhere to repent, because He has established a day on which He will judge the world in righteousness by the Man whom He has appointed. He has given assurance of this to everyone by raising Him from the dead." Acts 17:30-31

"But what does it say? The Word is near you, in your mouth and in your heart (that is, the Word of Faith which we preach): that if you confess with your mouth the Lord Jesus and believe in your heart that God has raised Him from the dead, you will be saved. For with the heart one believes unto righteousness, and with the mouth confession is made unto salvation." Romans 10:8-10

I would imagine that most people would scoff at such an idea. After all hasn't the 'churches' come out with new programs and are 'saving' droves of people. I tell you, take this as a SERIOUS warning beforehand, that most of those who proclaim to be Saved will be Left Behind, just as the vast majority of the members of their apostate churches, with all of their new and apostate programs! So with the backdrop of this discussion having been set, let's move along, for those who are still willing to read.

So the question then is who is the strong delusion for, if not the apostate church. For if you say that it is for the unsaved, those who wouldn't repeat a few words from a preacher to become 'saved', then note quite well that many people will be Saved during the Tribulation.

"After these things I looked, and behold, a great multitude which no one was able to number, of all nations, tribes, peoples, and tongues, standing before the throne and before the Lamb, clothed with white robes, with palm branches in their hands, and crying out with a loud voice, saying, Salvation belongs to our God who sits on the throne, and to the Lamb! And all the angels stood around the throne and the elders and the four living creatures, and fell on their faces before the throne and did homage to God, saying: Amen. Blessing and glory and wisdom, thanksgiving and honor and power and might, be to our God forever and ever. Amen. Then one of the elders answered, saying to me, Who are these arrayed in white robes, and where did they come from? And I said to him, Sir, you know. So he said to me, These are the ones coming out of great affliction, and have washed their robes and made them white in the blood of the Lamb. Therefore they are before the throne of God, and serve Him day and night in His temple. And He who sits on the throne will spread His tabernacle over them. They shall neither hunger anymore nor thirst anymore; the sun shall not fall on them, nor any burning heat; for the Lamb who is in the midst of the throne will shepherd them and lead them to living fountains of waters. And God will wipe away every tear from their eyes." Revelation 7:9-17

These will be those who repented and called out to the Lord to be Saved. They will not have been allowed by God to be deceived with a strong delusion.

"And it shall be, that whoever shall call on the name of Jehovah shall escape." Joel 2:32a

"For everyone, whoever calls on the name of the Lord shall be saved." Romans 10:13

These are those who, even during the *"time of Jacob's trouble" (Jer. 30:7)*, did not love their lives unto death, but rather became martyrs for Christ.

"And they overcame him through the blood of the Lamb and through the word of their testimony, and they did not love their lives unto death." Revelation 12:11

"And I saw thrones, and they sat on them, and judgment was committed to them; and I saw the souls of those who had been beheaded for their witness to Jesus and for the Word of God, who had not done homage to the beast or his image, and had not received his mark on their foreheads or on their hands. And they lived and reigned with Christ for a thousand years." Revelation 20:4

Yet the current apostate church can not even get the preaching right! If you say I am wrong, then where are all of these people in your congregations who have been 'saved' over the years. Where are your church members who are diligently doing what the Lord has stated, participating in the Great Commission *(Mk. 16:15)*? And for those who would say contrary, that you have them right now, come and see! I would suggest this:

Tear down your stages with lights, through away your instruments used to create rock and roll, preach the full Truth of the Bible. Talk about Creation as the Bible says so (six literal 24 hour days) *(Gen. 1)*, talk about the Flood being global *(Gen. 6-8)*, as the Bible does. Talk about a real Hell *(Matt. 25:46, Rev. 20:15)*, a place of eternal torment for those who are not Saved. Get rid of your fancy coffees, as an attraction to simply get people in the door to hear your false or watered down messages. Tell them to get right with God, to repent and allow God to make them Christ like, then you tell me what you have left!

If you can find one, go and look hard, they might be in your area, find a Church, like an independent fundamental Baptist Church that still preaches repentance, still has holy and sacred hymns sung, without the bells and whistles. Find this place who still has members who are serious about the things of God. They might be small, but they are rich *(Eph. 3:8)*. They might by puny in comparison to your big or bigger show, but they know God. If you still don't believe, then make a note, write it down. When the Rapture happens go back and visit. Perhaps there will be some individuals who will be Left Behind, but the Church will be gone. Either you will find yourself standing at the Judgment Seat of Christ *(2 Cor. 5:10)*, realizing that you had not rightly dividing the Word *(2 Tim. 2:15)* or you will have been Left Behind. This right here is the problem, take heed and pay attention!

Those who are Left Behind and thought they were Saved, but refused the Truth, now what? Now will they say people who said stuff like this were right, that such things were correct and now they are going to change their ways and go the right Way *(Jn. 14:6)*? Rather, take diligent heed for God Himself has said that they will be deceived and believe the lie, that He will send them a STRONG delusion. Therefore, God knowing the hearts *(Jer. 17:10)*, those who refused to repent and refused to believe, they will go along with the show, the reality is their souls are doomed to an eternity in the Lake of Fire *(Rev. 20:10-15)*! Do not let that be you!

So the question or the theory is out there. Could God allow the strong delusion to start prior to the Rapture?

A dear friend who worked in the ministry had pondered such a question years ago. People being prepped via television, the media and culture regarding alien life. Knowing that whatever truth lies with aliens is demonic, he pondered whether or not the governments of the world would utilize such a deception using holographic images, etc., to tell people after the Rapture had happened that aliens were the reason for it, etc. Basically a take off of Project Blue Beam, a possible scenario by the United States government. I take a look at things going on, being fairly well read, looking at what people are saying and I also ponder whether or not a deception of biblical proportions could be at hand. Could it be that the world is ripe for deception and God is allowing the groundwork to be laid to those who WILL BE deceived? Nonetheless, as of this publishing, the Rapture hasn't happened yet, so until then God is always willing for people to repent and accept Salvation through His Son, Jesus Christ.

"Beloved, I now write to you this second epistle (in both of which I stir up your pure minds by way of reminder), that you may remember the words which were spoken before by the holy prophets, and the commandment of us, the apostles of the Lord and Savior, knowing this first: that scoffers will come in the last days, walking according to their own lusts, and saying, Where is the promise of His coming? For since the fathers fell asleep, all things continue as they were since the beginning of creation. For of this they are willfully ignorant: that by the Word of God the heavens were of old, and the earth standing out of water and in the water, by which the world that then existed perished, being flooded with water. But the heavens and the earth which are now preserved by the same Word, are reserved for fire until the day of judgment and destruction of ungodly men. But, beloved, do not be unaware of this one thing, that with the Lord one day is as a thousand years, and a thousand years as one day. The Lord is not slow concerning His promise, as some count slowness, but is longsuffering toward us, not purposing that any should perish but that all should come to repentance. But the day of the Lord will come as a thief in the night, in which the heavens will pass away with a loud noise, and the elements will be dissolved with intense burning; both the earth and the works that are in it will be burned up." 2nd Peter 3:1-10

Amen!

Unprepared: Prepped Without Oil

"Then the kingdom of Heaven shall be likened to ten virgins who took their lamps and went out to meet the bridegroom. And five of them were wise, and five foolish. Those who were foolish took their lamps and took no oil with them, but the wise took oil in their vessels with their lamps. But while the bridegroom was delayed, they all nodded and fell asleep. And at midnight there was a cry: Behold, the bridegroom is coming; go out to meet him! Then all those virgins arose and prepared their lamps. And the foolish said to the wise, Give us some of your oil, for our lamps are going out. But the wise answered, saying, No, lest there should not be enough for us and you; but go rather to those who sell, and buy for yourselves. And while they went to buy, the bridegroom came, and those who were ready went in with him to the wedding feast; and the door was shut. Afterward the other virgins came also, saying, Lord, Lord, open to us! But he answered and said, Truly, I say to you, I do not know you. Watch therefore, for you know neither the day nor the hour in which the Son of Man comes." Matthew 25:1-13

I used to live in Kalispell, Montana. In Kalispell there are many liberty, freedom-minded people from all sorts of walks of life who live either in town or nearby in Flathead County. There is probably not a city in the United States, in terms of percentage of people, who are more liberty minded than those of Kalispell. On a regular basis you see pro 2nd Amendment, Oath Keepers, anti-Obama and other freedom themed bumper stickers. Chuck Baldwin also hosts a church here, called Liberty Fellowship, that has a decent following, considering that Kalispell is a small city.

Northwest Montana was in the news as the anchors were discussing how certain local real estate businesses are booming, people are buying second 'survival' homes in the rural areas. These houses are for those who don't live here, but with the assumption that at some point in time they might have to. Many of these houses are self-sufficient, off-the-grid, that are tucked away in areas far from the general population.

For years there had been renewed prepping calls by the alternative news community. The number of people who had determined to prep are in the millions and their preparations varied by each individual. The percentage was greater than those who prepped for the oil crisis and Y2K. There are many different theories as to what could happen, what will happen and situations that will likely arise, that present different philosophies about the likelihood of certain events.

People prepped for civil unrest, martial law, magnetic pole shifting, the apocalypse, the Tribulation, thermonuclear war, economic collapse and a variety of other reasons. I've known people who went from having a bit of extra food, candles, batteries and water to those who had 10,000 bolts (arrows), high tech thermal imaging cameras, numerous guns, large amount of ammo and food for years to come. Some harden their homes, putting plexiglass in, reinforcing doors and placing hidden bunkers on their property or hiding things in various places. There were those who prep with a camping mindset, to live off the land. Whatever the case, the varying degrees are astonishing.

A true Believer might have some items on hand as well or might have nothing extra at all. One thing a true Believer should never have is a seven year supply to supposedly survive the Tribulation (*"time of Jacob's trouble", Jer. 30:7*). For those who are truly His, He will come and gather us to Himself, prior to that time.

"For the Lord Himself will descend from Heaven with a shouted command, with the voice of the archangel, and with the trumpet of God. And the dead in Christ will rise first. Then we who are alive and remain shall be caught up together at the same time with them in the clouds to meet the Lord in the air. And thus we shall always be with the Lord." 1st Thessalonians 4:16-17

"Behold, I tell you a mystery: We shall not all sleep, but we shall all be changed; in a moment, in the twinkling of an eye, at the last trumpet. For the trumpet will sound, and the dead will be raised incorruptible, and we shall be changed." 1st Corinthians 15:51-52

"After these things I looked, and behold, a door having been opened in Heaven. And the first voice which I heard was like a trumpet speaking with me, saying, Come up here, and I will show you things which must take place after these things." Revelation 4:1

They state that Christians who believe in a pretrib Rapture, do not do anything to fight for freedom and liberty. They accuse us to be pacifists who are actually part of the problem and making the situation worse for all Americans. Well don't use me as an example in your arguments, because I would be in your 'gray' area and not fit in your argumentative mold.

In times past I spent a great deal of time trying to 'save' America. I partnered up with others and became heavily politically active, not only writing bombshell news articles to try and wake up the masses, but actively handing out information to the general public to try and get them to come to their senses. I also know more about prepping than the vast majority of people out there, having first hand knowledge. I did this not only as a Christian, but also as a pretrib Rapture believer. The reality is most people, whether they believe in pretrib, midtrib, posttrib or some concocted scheme, have not repented and believed into Jesus Christ. They are not part of the 'few' *(Mt. 7:14)*.

My reason for not 'fighting' for freedom anymore is the simple fact that this country has overall rejected God Almighty. In doing so, I do not wish to find myself in a -fight- against God by fighting for a country that refuses to not only repent of its' wrongdoings, but rather continues to push movements that go against God.

..."but if it is of God, you will not be able to overthrow it; lest you even be found to fight against God." Acts 5:39

"Thus says Jehovah the God of Israel: Behold, I will turn back the weapons of war that are in your hands, with which you fight against the king of Babylon, and against the Chaldeans who besiege you outside the walls. And I will gather them together in the

middle of this city. And I Myself will fight against you with an outstretched hand and with a strong arm, even in anger, and in fury, and in great wrath." Jeremiah 21:4-5

Here lies the problem with the vast majority of preppers, they are unprepared. Let me give you a couple of scenarios as to what would happen should the worst case scenario unfold.

There is a man I once conversed with, who has a place somewhere in Michigan. This man had his acreage, his rural setting and TONS of supplies. He is a fully trained law enforcement professional and could be considered a very sharp shooter. He literally has enough supplies to arm dozens of men and for that a prolonged battle. His plan included fortifying his home, being self-sufficient and able to defend his property. His conceived threat was the United States government would declare martial law, there would be an economic collapse and the fact that he would be wanted, as he was very outspoken against the federal government. This man not only is prepared, but he has trained thousands of people in prepping. He has a problem though.

If the situation is as bad as he surmises, and it may well one day be, a simple hellfire missile shot down his chimney would immediately render all of his preparations ineffective, as well as himself likely dead.

When I first moved to Montana in 2012, there were some who thought that we would certainly soon be in a situation that would require full activation. Indeed a few of them were already living in the wilderness. Yet I would interject some rare knowledge here about their plans.

Unbeknownst to most individuals, there are various border protecting and surveilling technologies used by the federal government, that would render most of the wilderness survivors ineffective. On national lands throughout the United States there are hidden metal detectors that set off an alarm when someone walks over one of them. If you were to pull up a Google satellite map and scour across the border to Canada (as many have spoke of fleeing to Canada) you will see that there is a swath of land that has been clear cut right along the border -- EXTENDING THE ENTIRE WOODED UNITED STATES, with the exception of Maine. In Maine that part of the border is privately owned.

Far overhead drones flyover, unseen to the eye, metal detectors signal border agents where to head to, cameras with lenses that can see for up to 100 miles (with no barriers) keep a close eye out, using the latest sophisticated software to detect human movement. Our northern border with Canada is MUCH more protected than most people know, even without an actual wall. The virtual wall has been put into place in the past dozen years and gets more high tech year after year. In the regular national forests, satellites can pick up every tree that falls and the slightest bit of smoke that rises into the air.

Needless to say, this is not simply the freedom minded people involved in prepping. The number of rich people building everything-proof bunkers, houses with high tech safe rooms and buying extremely rural multi-million dollar estates is impressive. There are many rich who have already prepared themselves second homes in far away countries, some have already resettled there. Then there are even those who simply live on luxury yachts, sailing the world, considering themselves to be independent of the system.

Maybe your one of the few who know these things and even more. Maybe your plan is far superior and you have backup after backup. Yet I would dare say the far-vast majority of people, no matter the complexity of their plan are simply: UNPREPARED.

Years ago in a local restaurant in Kalispell, I met with a group of people who mostly called themselves christians. Here the relevant news was discussed, people talked about prepping plans and became established with one another to create a network of help during the upcoming crisis. There were those who talked about using their home as a medical center, others would be supply houses, others would direct the men in battle and serve as commanders and numerous other scenarios. This group and the ones that it represented was not a fringe part of society, but rather reflected a percentage that could only be found in Kalispell.

As the talk filled the table and my wife and I listened, I could only note that not one person spoke about God, not one person spoke of ministering to people on behalf of Jesus, not one person spoke about the need for Salvation. On the contrary, God's name would be used in vain and no one seemed to even take notice, let alone blink an eye to the evil emitting from the perpetrators mouth. To make matters even worse, my wife and I walked outside the restaurant and noted three cars, with occupants, facing the restaurant, all with suspicious men who likely were FBI agents. When I addressed this matter to the group, one person out of them joined me in walking outside and viewing these people who were conceivably watching/listening to the conversations taking place, as well as recording license plates of the attendants. Shortly after a brief stare-down, all three of the cars (parked on the street or in different lots) left.

Of course these same patriots could not conceive that the very enemy that they were preparing to fight against could be amongst them, listening in, befriending them and taking part of the conversations. In all of history, has a military operation that has been compromised ever been successful. No nation willingly gives their enemy the battle plan prior to the battle, but rather uses the element of surprise to try and achieve their gains.

No matter the complexity of the plan, without Jesus your plan is null and void. Even if you were to take and be successful at every interval, when you eventually die, as all men die (*Hebrews 9:27*) you will stand before the Most High and unless you are in Christ, you will have met your Maker, unprepared. These preppers have no oil, they might name the name of Jesus, but in reality they are lost, unsaved and destined to Hell.

There is no hope for them in the afterlife, they have not the fear nor knowledge of God (*Pr. 9:10*). They do not know His Son, they have not repented of their sin. Understand that all of these preparations for the body are unfruitful if your soul is unprepared. This life is very short in comparison to eternity, but a blink of the eye. Most reading this will not be merely 18, but already much older, with an expected life span of 30-50 more years.

"And do not fear those who kill the body but are not able to kill the soul. But rather fear Him who has power to destroy both soul and body in Gehenna." Matthew 10:28

"Be anxious for nothing, but in everything by prayer and supplication, with thanksgiving, let your requests be made known to God; and the peace of God, which surpasses all understanding, will guard your hearts and minds in Christ Jesus." Philippians 4:6-7

"Therefore I say to you, do not be anxious about your life, what you will eat or what you will drink; nor about your body, what you will put on. Is not life more than food and the body more than clothing? Observe the birds of the air, for they neither sow nor reap nor gather into barns; yet your Heavenly Father feeds them. Are you not of more value than they? Which of you by being anxious is able to add one cubit to his stature? So why are you anxious about clothing? Consider the lilies of the field, how they grow: they neither toil nor spin; and yet I say to you that even Solomon in all his glory was not arrayed like one of these. Now if God so clothes the grass of the field, which today is, and tomorrow is thrown into the furnace, will He not much more clothe you, O you of little faith? Therefore do not be anxious, saying, What shall we eat? or What shall we drink? or What shall we wear? For after all these things the Gentiles seek. For your Heavenly Father knows that you need all these things. But seek first the kingdom of God and His righteousness, and all these things shall be added to you. Therefore do not be anxious about tomorrow, for tomorrow will worry about its own things. Sufficient for the day is its own trouble." Matthew 6:25-34

Maybe the worst case scenario unfolds, maybe you are indeed rounded up and placed in a concentration camp. Perhaps the economy collapses and your plans failed as you become quickly outnumbered by the desperate and hungry (have you seen what is happening in Venezuela?). Even so, the focus of this life, should not be the body, but rather the soul and rectifying your soul with your Creator through His Son Jesus Christ.

Regardless of where you standing on prepping, understand that without Jesus, whether you are rich or poor, prepped or unprepped, old or young, strong or weak, you are doomed. Consider your ways, consider your plans and understand the importance of biblical Salvation!

"Trust in Jehovah with all your heart, and lean not unto your own understanding. In all your ways acknowledge Him, and He shall direct your paths. Do not be wise in your own eyes; fear Jehovah and depart from evil." Proverbs 3:5-7

"Roll your ways upon Jehovah; trust also in Him, and He will bring it to pass. And He will bring forth your righteousness like the light, and your justice like the noonday. Rest in Jehovah, and wait patiently for Him; do not fret over him who prospers in his way, because of him who works out wicked devices. Cease from anger, and forsake wrath; do not fret; it only leads to evil. For evildoers shall be cut off; but those who wait upon

Jehovah, they shall inherit the earth. For yet a little while, and the wicked shall be no more; indeed, you shall diligently consider his place, and it shall be no more. But the lowly shall inherit the earth, and shall delight themselves in the abundance of peace. The wicked plots against the just, and gnashes at him with his teeth. Jehovah laughs at him, for He sees that his day is coming. The wicked have drawn out the sword and have bent their bow, to cast down the poor and needy, to slaughter those who walk uprightly. Their sword shall enter into their own heart, and their bows shall be broken. A little that the righteous has is better than the riches of many wicked. For the arms of the wicked shall be broken, but Jehovah upholds the righteous. Jehovah knows the days of the upright, and their inheritance shall be forever. They shall not be ashamed in the evil time, and in the days of famine they shall be satisfied. But the wicked shall perish, and the enemies of Jehovah shall be as prized lambs; they are consumed; like smoke they vanish." Psalms 37:5-20

Amen!

Repent!

"Jesus said, I tell you, no; but unless you repent you will all likewise perish." Luke 13:3

"And He said to them, Thus it is written, and thus it was necessary for the Christ to suffer and to rise from the dead the third day, and that repentance and remission of sins be preached in His name to all nations, beginning out of Jerusalem." Luke 24:46-47

There are churches all over from coast to coast of this country. Numerous different denominations, tons of different viewpoints on the Bible, where does one turn? What can be a test to see if these churches are biblical and truly have a pastor who is Saved and called by God to preach?

Doctrine is important, very important. There are numerous errors found throughout nearly every church across the United States, some more obvious than others. Some churches have some doctrines correct, others have other ones correct. While I am not speculating that anyone would find an absolutely perfect Church, the harsh reality is that a church where a biblical Salvation message is not preached, could simply not make sense regarding of how they are following Christ and adhering to doctrine.

The Bible is quite clear on doctrine and also provides some warnings to Believers regarding to check into what they hear, as well at times to go elsewhere, should you find yourself in the midst of wolves, or as often happens, a church changes slowly, becoming apostate *(Rev. 18:4)*.

"Till I come, give attention to reading, to exhortation, to doctrine." 1st Timothy 4:13

"Take heed to yourself and to the doctrine. Continue in them, for in doing this you will deliver both yourself and those who hear you." 1st Timothy 4:16

"These were more noble than those in Thessalonica, in that they received the Word with all readiness, and searched the Scriptures daily, to see whether these things are so." Acts 17:11

"I charge you therefore before God and the Lord Jesus Christ, who will judge the living and the dead at His appearing and His kingdom: Preach the Word. Be ready in season and out of season. Convict, rebuke, exhort, with all longsuffering and teaching. For the time will come when they will not endure sound doctrine, but according to their own lusts, desiring to hear pleasant things, they will heap up for themselves teachers; and they will turn their ears away from the truth, and be turned aside to myths. But you be watchful in all things, endure afflictions, do the work of an evangelist, fulfill your ministry." 1st Timothy 4:1-5

"Therefore, Come out from among them and be separate, says the Lord. Do not touch what is unclean, and I will receive you." 2nd Corinthians 6:17

While there are good Churches out there that do not hold to an Independent Fundamental Baptist name, truly I have always found the Independent Fundamental Baptists to be by far the closest and best to preaching Gospel truth. Yet even nowadays there are warning signs and red flags that are everywhere, including Baptists. Myself I would certainly just consider to be a saint of Jesus Christ, a true born-again Believer who has repented and by faith believed into Jesus Christ as my Lord and Savior.

I was Saved at the age of 9 in a Nazarene church in Alanson, Michigan. I do believe there are those who are Saved in numerous types of denominations. While the Roman Catholic Church certainly doesn't preach the true Gospel, but rather a works based, idolatrous pagan religion, certainly it would be possible for someone to get Saved *(Is. 55:11)* and find themselves attending there. Though a babe in Christ *(1 Cor. 3:1)*, one would think that sooner than later, the Holy Spirit would point out the error of the church they are in and they would be directed elsewhere.

The Bible is quite clear that repentance (more on this later) is necessary for Salvation. This used to be clearly indicated throughout Baptist churches way into the 1950's and then started a massive decline, effecting even the Independent Fundamental Baptist churches. I've spoken with many Independent Fundamental Baptist pastors regarding this ordeal.

Last year I met a retired pastor who was with his former congregation in Kalispell, Montana, where they were preaching on the street corner and handing out tracks. I happened to walk up to him and simply asked what one must do to be Saved. His reply, to the best of my knowledge, as people can have a play on the meaning of words, was biblical. He simply stated that one must repent and by faith believe in Jesus Christ. Unfortunately the church is under direction of a new pastor and their articles of faith are absent of even the word repentance. Why? How could the articles of faith on their website, as well as a vast majority of so-called Independent Fundamental Baptist churches, not include even the word repent?

Some might give a basic meaning, such as 'making a 180° turn', but most won't even do that. Certainly to tell a sinner that repentance, not simply faith, is necessary for Salvation won't attract large crowds. The unknown truth to the matter is often businessmen are on the boards of these churches, who employ the pastor. The outlook is for church growth, so the watering-down of God's Word, in order to not offend people, happens frequently. The idea behind such movements is that if they can get them into the church, they might be able to save them, but the truth is man doesn't Save, God does. Some claim that repentance is works, such nonsense, as a condition of someone's heart before God, could not be considered works, more than the mind working during prayer. Before we get more into this, taking a look from my old Webster's University dictionary of the meaning of repent and its varieties would be useful.

repent, v.i.
1) To feel pain, sorrow, or regret for something one has done or left undone.
2.) To change the mind in consequence of the inconvenience or injury done by past conduct.
3.) In theology, to feel such sorrow for sin as leads to amendment of life; to be penitent; to grieve over one's past life, and to seek forgiveness for sin, with a determination to lead a new life.

repent, v.t.
1.) To remember with sorrow, to feel contrition or remorse for; as, to repent rash words.
2.) To be sorry; to regret; used reflexively.
3.) To cause to have regret; used impersonally. (Obs.)

repentable, a.
Capable of being repented of; admitting of repentance.

repentance, n.
The act of repenting; the state of being penitent; sorrow or regret for what has been done or left undone by oneself; especially, sorrow and contrition for sin; such sorrow for the past as leads to amendment of life; penitence; contrition.

repentant, a.
1.) Feeling or experiencing repentance or sorrow for past conduct or words; contrite; penitent.
2.) Expressive of or indicating repentance or sorrow for the past; springing from or caused by repentance.

Webster's Universities Dictionary of the English Language, Noah Webster, 1942

Now, if one just simply pauses and comprehends what repentance is, then we will brush up on this in regards to sin. Quite simply put, repentance is realizing that one is worthy of God's Judgment for their sins, feeling sorrow and regret for their past sins and no longer wanting to do those things. Simply turning away from ones sins, changing their mind regarding sin and realizing that through the blood of Christ, Christ having paid their penalty for their sins, that they by faith believe into Jesus Christ as their Lord and Savior. We will brush up a bit more on Salvation in the end of this chapter, but first let's take a look at what the Bible says about repentance, for it is not silent, not in the least bit.

"Now after John was put in prison, Jesus came into Galilee, preaching the gospel of the kingdom of God, and saying, The time is fulfilled, and the kingdom of God is at hand. Repent, and believe in the gospel." Mark 1:14-15

"I know your works, that you are neither cold nor hot. I would that you were cold or hot. So then, because you are lukewarm, and neither cold nor hot, I will vomit you out of My mouth. Because you say, I am rich, have become wealthy, and have need of nothing; and do not know that you are wretched and miserable and poor and blind and naked; I

counsel you to buy from Me gold refined in the fire, that you may be rich; and white garments, that you may be clothed, that the shame of your nakedness may not be revealed; and anoint your eyes with eye salve, that you may see. As many as I love, I rebuke and chasten. Therefore be zealous and repent. Behold, I stand at the door and knock. If anyone hears My voice and opens the door, I will come in to him and dine with him, and he with Me. To him who overcomes I will grant to sit with Me on My throne, as I also overcame and sat down with My Father on His throne." Revelation 3:15-21*

"There was a certain rich man who was clothed in purple and fine linen and fared sumptuously every day. And there was a certain beggar named Lazarus, full of sores, who was laid at his gate, desiring to be fed with the crumbs which fell from the rich man's table. Moreover the dogs came and licked his sores. So it happened that the beggar died, and was carried by the angels into Abraham's bosom. The rich man also died and was buried. And being in torments in Hades, he lifted up his eyes and saw Abraham afar off, and Lazarus in his bosom. Then he cried and said, Father Abraham, have mercy on me, and send Lazarus that he may dip the tip of his finger in water and cool my tongue; for I am tormented in this flame. But Abraham said, Son, remember that in your lifetime you received your good things, and likewise Lazarus evil things; but now he is comforted and you are tormented. And besides all this, between us and you there is a great chasm fixed, so that those who want to pass from here to you are not able, nor can those from there pass to us. Then he said, I beg you therefore, father, that you would send him to my father's house, for I have five brothers, that he may testify to them, that they not also come to this place of torment. Abraham said to him, They have Moses and the Prophets; let them hear them. And he said, No, father Abraham; but if one goes to them from the dead, they will repent. But he said to him, If they do not hear Moses and the Prophets, neither will they be persuaded though one should rise from the dead." Luke 16:19-31*

"And He called the twelve to Himself, and began to send them out two by two, and gave them authority over unclean spirits, and commanded them to take nothing for the journey except a staff; no bag, no bread, no copper in their money belts; but to wear sandals, and not to put on two tunics. And He said to them, In whatever place you enter a house, stay there till you depart from that place. And whoever will not receive you nor hear you, when you depart from there, shake off the dust under your feet as a testimony against them. Truly, I say to you, it will be more tolerable for Sodom and Gomorrah in the day of judgment than for that city. So they went out and preached that people should repent." Mark 6:7-12*

"Then Peter said to them, Repent, and let every one of you be immersed in the name of Jesus Christ to the remission of sins; and you shall receive the gift of the Holy Spirit." Acts 2:38*

"But those things which God foretold through the mouth of all His prophets, that the Christ would suffer, He has thus fulfilled. Repent therefore and be converted, that your sins may be blotted out, so that times of refreshing may come from the presence of the Lord, and that He may send Jesus Christ, who was preached to you before, whom Heaven *must receive until the times of restoration of all things, of which God has spoken through the mouth of all His holy prophets since the past ages." Acts 3:18-21*

"Truly, these times of ignorance God overlooked, but now commands all men everywhere to repent, because He has established a day on which He will judge the world in righteousness by the Man whom He has appointed. He has given assurance of this to everyone by raising Him from the dead." Acts 17:30-31

"Therefore, King Agrippa, I was not disobedient to the Heavenly vision, but declared first to those in Damascus and in Jerusalem, and throughout all the region of Judea, and then to the Gentiles, that they should repent, turn to God, and do works befitting repentance." Acts 26:19-20

"I say to you that likewise there will be more joy in Heaven over one sinner who repents than over ninety-nine just persons who need no repentance. Or what woman, having ten silver coins, if she loses one coin, does not light a lamp, sweep the house, and search carefully until she finds it? And when she has found it, she calls her friends and neighbors together, saying, Rejoice with me, for I have found the piece which I lost! Likewise, I say to you, there is joy in the presence of the angels of God over one sinner who repents." Luke 15:7-10

"But go and learn what this means: I desire mercy and not sacrifice. For I did not come to call the righteous, but sinners, to repentance." Matthew 9:13

"The God of our fathers raised up Jesus whom you laid hands on, hanging Him on a tree. Him God has exalted to His right hand to be Prince and Savior, to give to Israel repentance and remission of sins. And we are His witnesses of these things, and so also is the Holy Spirit whom God has given to those who obey Him." Acts 5:30-32

"When they heard these things they kept silent; and they glorified God, saying, Then God has also granted to the Gentiles repentance unto life." Acts 11:18

"And when they had come to him, he said to them: You know, from the first day that I came to Asia, in what manner I lived among you all the time, serving the Lord with all humility, with many tears and trials which happened to me by the plotting of the Jews; how I kept back nothing that was helpful, but proclaimed it to you, and taught you publicly and from house to house, testifying both to Jews, and also to Greeks, repentance toward God and faith toward our Lord Jesus Christ." Acts 20:18-21

"But we know that the judgment of God is according to truth upon those who practice such things. And do you think this, O man, you who judges those practicing such things, and doing the same, that you will escape the judgment of God? Or do you despise the riches of His kindness, forbearance, and longsuffering, not knowing that the kindness of God leads you to repentance? But according to your hardness and impenitent heart you are treasuring up for yourself wrath in the day of wrath and revelation of the righteous judgment of God, who will render to each one according to his works: eternal life to

those who steadfastly doing good, seek for glory, honor, and incorruptibility; but to those who are self-seeking and do not obey the truth, but obey unrighteousness; anger and wrath, trouble and anguish, on every soul of man who produces evil, of the Jew first and also of the Greek; but glory, honor, and peace to everyone who works what is good, to the Jew first and also to the Greek. For there is no partiality with God." Romans 2:2-11

"Now I rejoice, not that you were made sorry, but that you were made sorry unto repentance. For you were made sorry in a godly manner, that you might suffer loss from us in nothing. For godly sorrow produces repentance leading to salvation, not to be regretted; but the sorrow of the world produces death. For observe this very thing, that you sorrowed in a godly manner: What diligence it produced in you, what clearing of yourselves, what indignation, what fear, what vehement desire, what zeal, what vengeance! In all things you proved yourselves to be clear in this matter." 2nd Corinthians 7:9-11

"But, beloved, do not be unaware of this one thing, that with the Lord one day is as a thousand years, and a thousand years as one day. The Lord is not slow concerning His promise, as some count slowness, but is longsuffering toward us, not purposing that any should perish but that all should come to repentance. But the day of the Lord will come as a thief in the night, in which the heavens will pass away with a loud noise, and the elements will be dissolved with intense burning; both the earth and the works that are in it will be burned up." 2nd Peter 3:8-10

Clearly it can be seen that the Bible is not silent on repentance. Repentance is part of Salvation, just as faith in Jesus Christ whom died on the Cross for our sins and rose again *(Eph. 1:20)*. By faith believing in Jesus, who is the Son of God, God in the flesh, whom God the Father sent, the free gift to all who will accept it.

"For by grace you are saved through faith; and that not of yourselves, it is the gift of God; not of works, that no one should boast." Ephesians 2:8-9

"Now it was not written for his sake alone, that it was accounted to him, but also for us, to whom it shall be accounted, believing in Him who raised up Jesus our Lord from the dead, who was delivered up because of our trespasses, and was raised for our justification." Romans 4:23-25

"For God so loved the world that He gave His only begotten Son, that everyone believing into Him should not perish but have eternal life. For God did not send His Son into the world to judge the world, but that the world through Him might be saved. The one believing into Him is not judged; but the one not believing is judged already, because he has not believed in the name of the only begotten Son of God. And this is the judgment, that the Light has come into the world, and men loved darkness rather than the Light, for their deeds were evil. For everyone practicing evil hates the Light and does not come to the Light, lest his deeds should be reproved. But the one doing the truth comes to the Light, that his deeds may be clearly seen, that they have been worked in God." John 3:16-21

"But God demonstrates His own love toward us, in that while we were yet sinners, Christ died for us." Romans 5:8

"Nor is there salvation in any other, for there is no other name under Heaven given among men that is required for us to be saved." Acts 4:12

"Jesus said to him, I am the Way, the Truth, and the Life. No one comes to the Father except through Me." John 14:6

"And he brought them out and said, Sirs, what must I do to be saved? So they said, Believe on the Lord Jesus Christ, and you will be saved, you and your household." Acts 16:30-31

"But what does it say? The Word is near you, in your mouth and in your heart (that is, the Word of Faith which we preach): that if you confess with your mouth the Lord Jesus and believe in your heart that God has raised Him from the dead, you will be saved. For with the heart one believes unto righteousness, and with the mouth confession is made unto salvation." Romans 10:8-10

"And as it is appointed for men to die once, and after this the judgment, so Christ was offered once to bear the sins of many. To those who eagerly wait for Him He will appear a second time, without sin, unto salvation." Hebrews 9:27-28

Understand that men water down the Word of God, but the Bible is quite clear regarding Salvation. Do not be deceived, while repentance might have gone missing from most pulpits around this country, certainly it hasn't gone missing from His Word.

Our job as Believers is to preach the Gospel, to tell people about Salvation, in a manner that is accurate in regards to the Holy Scriptures. Certainly we tell people that by faith that they are Saved *(Eph. 2:8-9)*, but we also tell them about repentance *(Acts 17:30-31)* or at least teach the essence of repentance, whether or not we use the word repent anywhere.

"Then Peter said to them, Repent, and let every one of you be immersed in the name of Jesus Christ to the remission of sins; and you shall receive the gift of the Holy Spirit." Acts 2:38

"The Lord is not slow concerning His promise, as some count slowness, but is longsuffering toward us, not purposing that any should perish but that all should come to repentance." 2nd Peter 3:9

"Repent therefore and be converted, that your sins may be blotted out, so that times of refreshing may come from the presence of the Lord,"... Acts 3:19

I have scoured tons of web pages of IFB churches and often look at their beliefs, as well as their Salvation message. While I am thankful that there are some here and there that preach Salvation as repent and believe, they are the minority. If it wasn't for preachers and ministries, like that of A Voice in the Wilderness *(www.a-voice.org)*, Way of Life *(www.wayoflife.org)* and others, I myself would question whether or not I was wrong on the issue. As many pastors I have talked to will either brush the topic or simply not give a clear answer, others will just say that repenting is not necessary.

There may be those pastors who are being carried away with such an apostate doctrine and are not even aware of what they are doing, despite the fact they themselves are Saved. Perhaps if they strongly considered it, they would realize that when they accepted Christ, they in essence repented, not by turning from unbelief to belief, but rather by realizing that they were a sinner *(Ro. 3:23)* and that they were guilty before a Holy and Almighty God *(Ro. 6:23)* and acknowledging that in their hearts, they also desired to change and no longer want to do those things *(Ro. 10:9)*, but they wanted to accept the free gift of Salvation *(Ro. 5:15)* and believed into Jesus Christ as their Lord and Savior *(Ro. 10:10)*. For certainly one can not say that someone can not be Saved with a sinner's prayer, as it is a heart issue, a matter of the individual before God almighty. Though the 'sinner's prayer' is not found anywhere in the Bible and I personally would never recommend using it, but dealing with each individual, as an individual.

Recall it is repentance towards God and faith in Christ Jesus. So let's just cut to the chase regarding this matter of believe only.

"You believe that God is One. You do well. Even the demons believe, and shudder." Jacob (James) 2:19

So why not take it to the full extreme. Let's just go ahead and go with what many churches teach:

"So they said, Believe on the Lord Jesus Christ, and you will be saved, you and your household." Acts 16:31

So we will ignore the fact that the text of the passage would very strongly suggest that the jailer had repented in his heart towards God prior to asking about how to be Saved. I've been in the South Side of Chicago off and on for years and know that there are some churches around there that simply state:

"For everyone, whoever calls on the name of the Lord shall be saved." Romans 10:13

They ignore the verses right before that verse:

"But what does it say? The Word is near you, in your mouth and in your heart (that is, the Word of Faith which we preach): **that if you confess with your mouth the Lord Jesus** _and_ **believe in your heart that God has raised Him from the dead, you will be saved. For with the heart one believes unto righteousness,** _and_ **with the mouth**

confession is made unto salvation. *For the Scripture says, Everyone believing on Him will not be put to shame. For there is no distinction between Jew and Greek, for the same Lord over all is rich toward all who call upon Him." Romans 10:8-12*

So why make things so complex. While some pastors would shy away from going door to door with a weak Gospel message and trying to get someone to repeat a prayer, instantly stating that they are Saved, many others will not. Is it really that simple? Well Salvation is simple *(Acts. 20:21)*, but the problem is men don't want to repent *(Rev. 9:21)*. So taking away that mandate I ask this: Why not simply take and go out there and just briefly explain to people who Jesus was and is *(John 1:1)*, telling them that if they believe in Him *(Acts 16:31)*, that He is the Son of God *(John 20:31)*, who died on the Cross for their sins *(1 Pet. 2:24)* and rose again from the dead *(Ro. 6:4)*, that they also can be Saved.

Simply put, you explain it to someone, tell them that they can know for sure where they go when they die and ask them if they believe. Why even have them pray about it? At that point, as long as they seemed to sincerely believe, what difference would it make if they continued on their lives living in absolute sin and never once contemplated the things of God?

Well you see, that is exactly what most are going to do, because they haven't repented. While from time to time they might think about the things of God, they are going to live their life, without surrendering to Jesus Christ as their Lord and Savior. And far be it from me to be one who tells such a person that they are for sure (giving them assurance when I do not know the heart) going to go to Heaven when they die, despite their lives not having any evidence of being changed!

Imagine watching as someone who you witnessed to and proclaimed to be Saved stands before the Great White Throne *(Rev. 20:11-15)*, being cast into the Lake of Fire for all eternity! What sorrow and despair, for but a moment, as you stand at the judgment Seat of Christ *(2 Cor. 5:10)*, knowing that that man who will stand before the Creator *(Ro. 14:12)* is doomed for all eternity and you assured him that he was not! This is serious business! Is it any wonder that Jesus said the following:

"Enter by the narrow gate; for wide is the gate and broad is the way that leads to destruction, and there are many entering in through it. Because narrow is the gate and distressing is the way which leads unto life, and there are few who find it. Beware of false prophets, who come to you in sheep's clothing, but inwardly they are ravenous wolves. You will know them from their fruits. Do men gather grapes from thornbushes or figs from thistles? Even so, every good tree produces excellent fruit, but a corrupt tree produces evil fruit. A good tree is not able to produce evil fruit, nor is a corrupt tree able to produce excellent fruit. Every tree that does not produce excellent fruit is cut down and thrown into the fire. Therefore from their fruits you will know them. Not everyone who says to Me, Lord, Lord, will enter the kingdom of Heaven, but he who does the will of My Father in Heaven. Many will say to Me in that day, Lord, Lord, have we not prophesied in Your name, cast out demons in Your name, and done many works of power

in Your name? And then I will declare to them, I never knew you; depart from Me, you who work out lawlessness!" Matthew 7:13-23

So I ask you, which of these didn't believe! Those who cast out demons, those who did works of power in His name or those who prophesied in His name? Answer me that.

Amen!

President Trump - A Perfect Example

"And then the lawless one will be unveiled, whom the Lord will consume with the breath of His mouth and destroy with the brightness of His coming. The coming of the lawless one is according to the working of Satan, with all power, signs, and lying wonders, and with all unrighteous deception among those who are perishing, because they did not receive the love of the truth, that they might be saved. And for this reason God will send them strong delusion, that they should believe the lie, that they all may be judged who did not believe the truth but had pleasure in unrighteousness." 2nd Thessalonians 2:8-12

"But of that day and hour no one knows, not even the angels of Heaven, but My Father only. But as the days of Noah were, so also will the coming of the Son of Man be. For as in the days before the flood, they were eating and drinking, marrying and giving in marriage, until the day that Noah entered into the ark, and did not realize until the flood came and took them all away, so also will the coming of the Son of Man be. Then two will be in the field: one is taken and the other is left. Two will be grinding at the mill: one is taken and the other is left. Watch therefore, for you do not know what hour your Lord comes. But know this, that if the master of the house had known what hour the thief comes, he would have watched and not allowed his house to be dug through. Therefore you also be ready, for the Son of Man comes at an hour you do not expect. Who then is a faithful and wise servant, whom his master made administrator over his household, to give them food in due season? Blessed is that servant whom his master, when he comes, will find so doing. Truly, I say to you that he will appoint him as administrator over all his possessions. But if that wicked servant says in his heart, My master delays his coming, and begins to beat his fellow servants, and to eat and drink with the drunkards, the master of that servant will come on a day when he is not expecting him and in an hour he does not know, and will cut him in two and appoint him his portion with the hypocrites. There shall be weeping and gnashing of teeth." Matthew 24:36-51

Emphasis needs to be placed on the fact that NO ONE will know who the Antichrist is before the Rapture. However, in 2nd Thessalonians 2:8, the Antichrist is going to be unveiled after the Rapture. Now, would this not suggest that the Antichrist is already in the process of rising to power??? Would there not be a generation that would be living, with the man of sin on the scene, not yet unveiled, even if not suspected by the far vast majority???

The implications here regarding the Strong Delusion that is sent by God, is the fact that those who are deceived, will remain deceived all the way to the Lake of Fire *(Rev. 20:15)*. Unfortunately President Donald Trump provides a perfect example of how the Antichrist could rise to power and no one would know it.

In fact, President Trump's presidency is full of evangelical so-called christians who would never suspect President Trump of being a potential candidate for the Antichrist. Rather than suspecting him of being the Antichrist, they assign him with being sent by God. President Trump has been compared to numerous biblical figures, including Jesus Christ. He has been said to be like Elijah, Moses, Jesus, the second coming of God, the

King of Israel, as well as having been referenced by the Laodicean church *(Rev. 3:14-22)* as sent by God or being used by God. Are not these same people who call themselves christians part of the lukewarm church that WILL be spewed out of God's mouth, also those who will be deceived by the Strong Delusion?

If not them, then who? The leftist and alt-left who practice and love abortion, Antifa, etc. No, rather what does Christ say to the Laodicean church? Repent!

"And to the angel of the church of the Laodiceans write, These things says the Amen, the Faithful and True Witness, the Beginning of the creation of God: I know your works, that you are neither cold nor hot. I would that you were cold or hot. So then, because you are lukewarm, and neither cold nor hot, I will vomit you out of My mouth. Because you say, I am rich, have become wealthy, and have need of nothing; and do not know that you are wretched and miserable and poor and blind and naked; I counsel you to buy from Me gold refined in the fire, that you may be rich; and white garments, that you may be clothed, that the shame of your nakedness may not be revealed; and anoint your eyes with eye salve, that you may see. As many as I love, I rebuke and chasten. Therefore be zealous and repent. Behold, I stand at the door and knock. If anyone hears My voice and opens the door, I will come in to him and dine with him, and he with Me. To him who overcomes I will grant to sit with Me on My throne, as I also overcame and sat down with My Father on His throne. He who has an ear, let him hear what the Spirit says to the churches. " Revelation 3:14-22

President Trump provides the perfect example of how far apostate the condition of the church age is and just how the Antichrist could rise to power. Furthermore, if President Trump or anyone else like him ever turned out to actually be the Antichrist, it is quite apparent how the Strong Delusion could already be in effect -prior- to the Rapture of those who truly know Jesus Christ. Take heed!

Years ago churches for the most part quit talking about end times event. Perhaps this mindset came into play:

"Beloved, I now write to you this second epistle (in both of which I stir up your pure minds by way of reminder), that you may remember the words which were spoken before by the holy prophets, and the commandment of us, the apostles of the Lord and Savior, knowing this first: that scoffers will come in the last days, walking according to their own lusts, and saying, Where is the promise of His coming? For since the fathers fell asleep, all things continue as they were since the beginning of creation." 2nd Peter 3:1-4

Whereas originally many Baptist Churches would preach about the Rapture, the Tribulation, the Antichrist, the Second Coming, the Millennial Kingdom, as well as Hell, they have moved along from these topics. There were also other churches that taught the same sort of things, sometimes in different regards. However, now if one were to attend the vast majority of churches, if even the Rapture was mentioned in a sermon, it would most times be incorrectly stated that it wouldn't happen until the end of the seven year

Tribulation, which would be more aptly named the *"time of Jacob's trouble" (Jer. 30:7)* or simply the Seventh Week *(Da. 9:27)*.

Here we are in 2020, where those who call themselves Christians should be watching and ready, they simply are not.

"The harvest is past, the summer is ended, and we are not saved." Jeremiah 8:20

How long before it is too late! The job as Believers is not to try and guess who the Antichrist is, however interesting those things may or may not be. But what happens when someone is rising to power and meeting the criteria AS LAID OUT IN THE HOLY SCRIPTURES?! Or at least appears to be able to fulfill those things! Should nothing be said, should it not at least be pointed out?

To make matters worse, when someone, like President Trump, has potential similarities of the prophesized Antichrist and the lukewarm church throughout America (and much of the world) are looking at him as coming from God! Will not the Antichrist appear to be a 'good' guy?

"For such are false apostles, deceitful workers, transforming themselves into apostles of Christ. And no wonder; for Satan himself transforms himself into an angel of light. Therefore it is no great thing if his ministers also transform themselves into ministers of righteousness, whose end will be according to their works." 2nd Corinthians 11:13-15

Too many Hollywood movies have depicted the Antichrist as essentially a man who has devil horns coming out of his head, clearly evil. Yet, what if the Antichrist rises unto the scenes appearing to be a minister of righteousness? Do not be deceived, nor think that once it is known for sure you will correct your thoughts. For if God allows you to be deceived by the Strong Delusion because you did not receive the love of the truth, your fate is sealed, you are CERTAIN to end up in the Lake of Fire. No! Now is the time to not try and prove who the Antichrist is or be convinced about President Trump as the Antichrist, but RATHER for YOU to get right with God. For YOU to repent and by faith believe into Jesus Christ as your Lord and Savior, having your name written in the Book of Life.

For even if you were not part of those who deservingly are sent the Strong Delusion by God, know this, when you have enough evidence to prove whoever the Antichrist might be, will you even have made it that far through the *"time of Jacob's trouble" (Jer. 30:7)*. I've stated it before and I will say it again.

Even if one prepped out and had everything they needed and were somehow able to make it through the Tribulation, still, even if they lived until 100, when they die, without Christ, there is NO HOPE. So exactly what is the point? What are you waiting for? Do you not know that Christ died for your sins? Do you not realize that all have sinned, INCLUDING you? Do you not realize that the wages of sin is death? Do you not realize that there is not only Heaven, but also Hell, both of which are eternal? When will you decide to forsake your wicked ways and turn aside from them, repenting towards God and by faith accepting Christ?

"For He says: In an acceptable time I have heard you, and in a day of salvation I have helped you. Behold, now is the accepted time; behold, now is the day of salvation." 2nd Corinthians 6:2

..." for all have sinned and fall short of the glory of God,"... Romans 3:23

"For the wages of sin is death, but the gift of God is eternal life in Christ Jesus our Lord." Romans 6:23

"Do not marvel at this; for the hour is coming in which all who are in the graves will hear His voice and come forth; those who have done good, unto the resurrection of life, and those who have practiced evil, unto the resurrection of judgment." John 5:28-29

"Let the wicked forsake his way, and the unrighteous man his thoughts; and let him return to Jehovah, and He will have mercy on him; and to our God, for He will abundantly pardon." Isaiah 55:7

"But what does it say? The Word is near you, in your mouth and in your heart (that is, the Word of Faith which we preach): that if you confess with your mouth the Lord Jesus and believe in your heart that God has raised Him from the dead, you will be saved. For with the heart one believes unto righteousness, and with the mouth confession is made unto salvation. For the Scripture says, Everyone believing on Him will not be put to shame. For there is no distinction between Jew and Greek, for the same Lord over all is rich toward all who call upon Him. For everyone, whoever calls on the name of the Lord shall be saved." Romans 10:8-13

"Truly, these times of ignorance God overlooked, but now commands all men everywhere to repent, because He has established a day on which He will judge the world in righteousness by the Man whom He has appointed. He has given assurance of this to everyone by raising Him from the dead." Acts 17:30-31

I'm sure this is -too much religion- for way too many people. People want to hear the facts or so-called facts, they want to see the evidence, but of what avail is it to someone if they do not get Saved? President Trump provides a perfect example of just how many people could be Left Behind and be part of God's Strong Delusion. While some very interesting quotes will be pointed out momentarily regarding President Trump and how he could match the biblical description of the Antichrist, please note that the purpose of this chapter is not to prove that President Trump could be a realistic candidate for the Antichrist, but rather to prove just how lost the world is and how easily it could be deceived, especially that which calls itself christian.

While I certainly don't expect to make waves and for the big churches to suddenly abandon ship of all of their false doctrine, repent and get right with God, truly serving

Jesus Christ, I do hope that those who will hear will understand that they as individuals will stand before their Creator and they will not be able to lean on these false churches, but must come out and serve God wholeheartedly.

"And I heard another voice from Heaven saying, Come out of her, my people, so that you not share in her sins, and so that you not receive of her plagues." Revelation 18:4

I've scoured the internet for articles that talk about President Trump being the Antichrist and have found few. The few that I did find use numerology, pagan works or are just plain old nonsense. All of them have one thing in common, they say for certain that President Trump is the Antichrist. The Bible says that the man of sin is NOT unveiled until after the Rapture *(2 Thes. 2:8)*, so NO ONE could know for certain about anyone being the Antichrist.

However, unlike others, there is no need to turn to pagan works or numerology to make a case for President Trump being a potential candidate for the Antichrist. Simply using the Bible, as I did with the chapter on the Antichrist, could provide sufficient information to make him a perfect example of what a potential candidate of the Antichrist might look like. A candidate might look just like President Trump. Let's take a look at some of the characteristics of the Antichrist and ponder, a hypothesis, as to whether or not President Trump would line up, according to what the Bible states.

Please note, that while it is pondered here what perhaps the Bible means regarding these characteristics, much of this is sealed until the end and will simply not be known until that time.

"But you, O Daniel, shut up the words and seal the book, to the time of the end. Many shall run to and fro, and knowledge shall be increased." Daniel 12:4

First let's take a look at the revived Roman empire and ask, pondering a few things, not knowing for sure, but simply asking, could it be?

"And another sign appeared in the heavens: behold, a great, fiery red dragon having seven heads and ten horns, and seven diadems on his heads." Revelation 12:3

"And after this I was looking in the night visions. And, behold, the fourth beast was frightening and terrifying, and very strong! And it had great iron teeth. It devoured, and broke in pieces, and stamped what was left with its feet. And it was different from all the beasts before it; and it had ten horns. I was contemplating the horns. And behold, another little horn came up among them, and three of the first horns were uprooted before it. And behold, in this horn were eyes like the eyes of a man, and a mouth speaking great things. I watched until the thrones were cast down, and the Ancient of Days sat, whose robe was white as snow and the hair of His head like pure wool. His throne was like flames of fire, its wheels like burning fire. A stream of fire went out and came out from before Him. A thousand thousands served Him, and a vast innumerable number stood before Him. The judgment was set and the books were opened. Then I was

watching because of the voice of the great words which the horn spoke. I was watching until the beast was killed, and his body was destroyed and given to the burning flame. As for the rest of the beasts, their dominion was taken away. Yet their lives were prolonged for a season and a time. I saw in the night visions. And behold, one *like the Son of Man came with the clouds of the heavens. And He came to the Ancient of Days. And they brought Him near before Him. And dominion was given to Him, and glory, and a kingdom, that all peoples, nations, and languages should serve Him. His dominion is* an *everlasting dominion which shall not pass away, and His kingdom that which shall not be destroyed. I, Daniel, was distressed in my spirit within my body, and the visions of my head troubled me. And I came near one of those who stood by and asked him the truth of all this. So he told me and made me know the interpretation of the things. These great beasts which are four,* are *four kings which shall rise up out of the earth. But the saints of the Most High shall receive the kingdom and possess the kingdom forever, even forever and ever. Then I wanted to know the truth of the fourth beast, which* was *different from all of the others, very frightening, with its teeth of iron and its nails of bronze;* which *devoured and broke in pieces, and trampled what was left with its feet, also of the ten horns that* were *on its head, and the other which came up, and before whom three fell, even that horn that* had *eyes, and a mouth speaking great things, whose appearance* was *greater than his fellows. I was watching, and the same horn made war with the saints and prevailed against them, until the Ancient of Days came. And judgment was given to the saints of the Most High, and the time came that the saints possessed the kingdom. And he said, The fourth beast shall be the fourth kingdom on earth, which shall be different from all other kingdoms, and shall devour the whole earth, and shall trample it down and break it in pieces. And the ten horns out of this kingdom* are *ten kings; they shall rise, and another shall rise after them. And he shall be different from the first, and he shall abase three kings." Daniel 12:7-24*

"And in your place shall arise another kingdom inferior to yours, and another third kingdom of bronze, which shall rule over all the earth. And the fourth kingdom shall be as *strong as iron. Inasmuch as iron breaks in pieces and shatters all things, and like iron that crushes all these, it will break in pieces and crush. And whereas you saw the feet and the toes, partly of potters' clay and partly of iron,* the *kingdom shall be divided. But there shall be in it the strength of iron, just as you saw the iron mixed with miry clay. And* as *the toes of the feet* were *partly of iron and partly of clay,* so *the kingdom shall be partly strong and partly broken. And as you saw the iron mixed with the miry clay, they shall become mixed with the seed of men. But they shall not cleave to one another, even as iron does not fellowship with clay. And in the days of these kings, the God of Heaven shall set up a kingdom which shall never be destroyed. And the kingdom shall not be left to other people. It shall break in pieces and bring all these kingdoms to an end, and it shall stand forever." Daniel 2:39-44*

"In the third year of the reign of King Belshazzar, a vision appeared to me, Daniel, after that which appeared to me the first time. And I saw in the vision, and it happened when I looked that I was *at Shushan, the palace, which* is *in the province of Elam. And in the vision I saw that I was by the Ulai River. Then I lifted up my eyes and looked. And behold, a ram was standing before the river,* having *horns. And the horns* were *high, but*

one was *higher than the other, and the higher one came up last. I saw the ram pushing westward and northward and southward, so that no beasts could stand before him, and no one could deliver out of his hand. But he did according to his will and became great. And as I was considering, behold, a male goat came from the west, over the face of the whole earth and did not touch the ground. And the he goat* had *a conspicuous horn between his eyes. And he came to the ram with* the *horns which I had seen standing before the river, and ran at him with furious power. And I saw him come close to the ram. And he was enraged against him. And* he *struck the ram and broke his two horns. And there was no power in the ram to stand before him. But he threw him down to the ground and trampled him. And there was no one that could deliver the ram from his hand. Then the male goat became very great. And when he became strong, the great horn was broken. And in its place came up four conspicuous ones toward the four winds of the heavens. And out of one of them came a little horn which became very great, toward the south, and toward the east, and toward the beautiful* land. *And it became great,* even *to the host of the heavens. And it caused some of the host and of the stars to fall to the ground, and trampled them. He magnified himself even to the Prince of the host. And the regular* sacrifice *was taken away by him, and the foundation of His sanctuary was cast down. And a host was assigned* to him *against the regular* sacrifice *because of transgression. And he cast truth down to the ground. He did* all this *and prospered. Then I heard a certain holy one speaking, and another holy one said to the one who spoke, For how long is the vision,* concerning *the regular* sacrifice *and the transgression of desolation, to permit both the holy place and the host to be trampled? And he said to me, For two thousand three hundred evenings and mornings; then the holy place will be put right. And it happened when I, Daniel, had seen the vision, and sought the understanding, that behold, one having the appearance of a man stood before me. And I heard a man's voice between* the banks of *Ulai, and he called and said, Gabriel, make this one understand the vision. And he came near where I stood. And when he came, I was afraid and fell on my face. But he said to me, O son of man, understand that the vision* is *about the time of the end. And while he was speaking with me, I was in a deep sleep with my face toward the ground. But he touched me, and stood me upright. And he said, Behold, I will make you know what shall happen at the time of the end of the indignation. For at the appointed time the end* will come. *The ram which you saw with* two *horns* are *the kings of Media and Persia. And the male goat* is *the king of Greece. And the great horn between his eyes is the first king. And as for that which was broken, and four stood up in its place, four kingdoms shall stand up out of the nation, but not in its power. And in the latter time of their kingdom, when the transgressors have come to the full, a king shall stand forth, having fierce countenance and understanding sinister schemes. And his power shall be mighty, but not by his own power. And he shall destroy extraordinarily, and he shall prosper, and work, and destroy the mighty and the holy people. And also through his cunning he will cause deceit to prosper in his hand. And he will magnify himself in his heart, and through prosperity shall destroy many. He shall also stand up against the Ruler of rulers, but he shall be broken in pieces without hands. And the morning and evening vision that was told* is *true. But you shall close up the vision, for it* is yet *for many days. And I, Daniel, fainted and was sick* for *days. Afterward, I got up and did the king's business. And I was astonished at the vision, but did not understand* it." *Daniel 8*

So exactly what where the four kingdoms? The first was the Babylonian, the second was the Medo-Persian, the third was the Greek and the fourth was the Roman. Generally, at least it used to be, among fundamental Christian Churches, particularly Baptists, it is commonly believed that Daniel speaks of the revived Roman empire. I personally believe from my study of the Bible that to be exactly true. There are some who say that all of these things have already happened, but common sense should prevail that this is certainly not the case. Other arguments regarding what these things mean, alternative viewpoints, can be readily debunked using the Word of God.

The evidence stands that right now we are living in the times of the revived Roman empire. Where is it? Where is it headquarters? Well that could be up for debate, but there are some very interesting things. The Club of Rome broke the world into ten different kingdoms. Though they are called regional groups or otherwise, the point is the world is currently broke into ten regions. Consider:

"And as the toes of the feet were partly of iron and partly of clay, so the kingdom shall be partly strong and partly broken." Daniel 2:42

Clearly there are still some areas of the world that have lacked economic prowess and development. Consider Africa for an example. Africa is a far cry from civilization in Europe, in terms of prosperity and overall functionality. The poverty level of Africa should say enough. Could it be that we are living in a time, and by the way have been, that these things are right here, yet preachers from the pulpits rarely talk about such thing?

Another figment of Hollywood's imagination when it comes to the end times, the Antichrist, etc., is that the Antichrist will instantly be ruling over everything. Essentially the Rapture happens and suddenly the Antichrist is on the scene ruling everything. Well consider this:

"And the ten horns out of this kingdom are ten kings; they shall rise, and another shall rise after them. And he shall be different from the first, and he shall abase three kings." Daniel 7:24

If the Antichrist shall abase three kings, then would that not suggest that his rise to power is not necessarily immediately and without a fight? So some basic questions, going back and forth continuing on this chapter, have to be asked.

In order for the Antichrist to abase three kings, would he not need a powerful military, whether via threat or actual intervention? Would one consider that the Antichrist would rise out of a country like Bolivia? Could Bolivia control the world or would there threats work? Now in the current scope of things it is apparent that the way the world is setup, it would seem feasible for the Antichrist to come from a country where there is a strong military.

This is not to say that perhaps right now we are not living in the timeframe spoken of by Daniel. Perhaps 200 years from now, long after we are all gone and while our individual decisions regarding truly accepting Christ as our Savior will have been sealed, the world is a different place and a country that does not even exist at the moment is what will become the revived Roman empire. Yet the Bible clearly says to be "watching and ready". So while in this body, in this lifetime, serving Christ wholeheartedly, one should be watching AND ready *(Matt. 24:42-44)*.

"But take heed to yourselves, lest your hearts be weighed down with giddiness, drunkenness, and cares of this life, and that Day come upon you unexpectedly. For it will come as a snare on all those who dwell on the face of the whole earth. Watch therefore, and pray always that you may be counted worthy to escape all these things that will come to pass, and to stand before the Son of Man." Luke 21:34-36

Another thing to take into consideration is the following:

"And he cried mightily with a loud voice, saying, Babylon the great is fallen, is fallen, and has become a dwelling place of demons, a prison for every unclean spirit, and a cage for every unclean and hated bird! For all the nations have drunk of the wine of the wrath of her sexual perversities, the kings of the earth have prostituted themselves with her, and the merchants of the earth have become rich through the power of her luxury. And I heard another voice from Heaven saying, Come out of her, my people, so that you not share in her sins, and so that you not receive of her plagues. For her sins have reached to Heaven, and God has remembered her iniquities. Render to her just as she rendered to you, and repay her double according to her works; in the cup which she has mixed, mix double for her. By however much she has glorified herself and lived luxuriously, by the same amount give her torment and sorrow; for she says in her heart, I sit as queen, and am no widow, and will not see sorrow. Therefore her plagues will come in one day; death and mourning and famine. And she will be consumed with fire, for strong is the Lord God who judges her. The kings of the earth who prostituted themselves and lived luxuriously with her will weep and lament for her, when they see the smoke of her burning, standing at a distance because of the terror of her torment, saying, Alas, alas, that great city Babylon, that mighty city! For in one hour your judgment has come. And the merchants of the earth will weep and mourn over her, for no one buys their merchandise anymore: merchandise of gold and silver, precious stones and pearls, fine linen and purple, silk and scarlet, every kind of thyine wood, every kind of object of ivory, every kind of object of most precious wood, bronze, iron, and marble; and cinnamon and incense, ointment and frankincense, wine and oil, fine flour and wheat, beasts and sheep, horses and chariots, and bodies and souls of men. And the fruit that your soul lusted for has gone from you, and all the things which are rich and splendid have gone from you, and you shall find them no more at all. The merchants of these things, who became rich by her, will stand at a distance because of the terror of her torment, weeping and wailing, and saying, Alas, alas, that great city that was clothed in fine linen, purple, and scarlet, and adorned with gold and precious stones and pearls! For in one hour such great riches is come to nothing. Every shipmaster, all who travel by ship, sailors, and as many as trade on the sea, stood at a distance and cried out when they saw the smoke of her burning, saying, What is like this great city? And they threw dust on their heads and cried out, weeping and wailing, and saying, Alas, alas, that great city, in which all who

had ships on the sea became rich by her wealth! For in one hour she is made desolate. Rejoice over her, O Heaven, and you holy apostles and prophets, for God has avenged you on her! Then a mighty angel took up a stone like a great millstone and threw it into the sea, saying, Thus with violence the great city Babylon shall be thrown down, and shall by no means be found anymore. The sound of harpists, musicians, flutists, and trumpeters shall by no means be heard in you anymore. No craftsman of any craft shall ever be found in you anymore, and the sound of a millstone shall by no means be heard in you anymore. And the light of a lamp shall not ever shine in you anymore, and the voice of bridegroom and bride shall not ever be heard in you anymore. For your merchants were the great men of the earth, for by your sorcery all the nations were led astray. And in her was found the blood of prophets and saints, and of all who were slain on the earth." Revelation 18:2-24*

Now some might be quick to say that this cannot be America. Revelation 18 deals with the SAME timeframe as the *"time of Jacob's trouble" (Jer. 30:7)*. I don't know about you, but at this current stage of world history, I'm not worried about Italy, nor does it yet seem feasible that Europe has the prowess to fulfill this. It should be noted, just because commercial Babylon will be destroyed, does not mean it will happen in the beginning of the 7 year Tribulation, it may very well be towards the very end. Let me interject another verse that -could- be talking about Americans.

"In that time the present shall be brought to Jehovah of Hosts from a nation tall and smooth, from a people to be feared until now *and onward; a mighty nation, treading underfoot; whose land the rivers have divided; to the place of the name of Jehovah of Hosts, Mount Zion." Isaiah 18:7*

Nonetheless, for the sake of argument, certainly the apostasy is in full bloom right now. The world is getting worse and worse, just a daily reading of news events show that this is happening. Even those who don't proclaim to be Christians are aware that things are getting bad.

"But evil men and pretenders will grow worse and worse, leading astray and being led astray." 2nd Timothy 3:13

"But as the days of Noah were, so also will the coming of the Son of Man be." Matthew 24:37

"The earth also was corrupt before God, and the earth was filled with violence. And God looked upon the earth, and behold it was corrupt; for all flesh had corrupted their way upon the earth." Genesis 6:11-12

Certainly being Saved, watching and ready is what each individual should be doing, though they are not. Whether or not we live in such times right now or if it will be a future generation, the basis for this writing is that the world is ripe right now and possibly setup for a Strong Delusion. If that is the case now, how much more later on?

As will be discussed a bit more, it is known that the Antichrist will be a military man, heading a powerful military *(Rev. 13:4)*. Looking at the current geopolitical schemes of things, that would limit the current countries or political alignments to three. The United States of America, Russia and China.

Now all three things have one thing in common, it is possible to mutually destroy each other. Winning is really losing, who could determine a winner between such powerful weaponry. Yet if we consider that commercial Babylon, as I like to call it corporate Babylon, is somehow tied into the revived Roman empire, than it simply leaves two, the United States of America and China.

The odd thing about the United States is this ongoing rumor that the United States was designed to bring in the new world order. I would rather say that ultimately the new world order is simply a synonym for the Antichrist world government system or rather revived Roman empire. While China is becoming more powerful, truly the United States is still the economic powerhouse of the world.

While there would be some who would be quick to point out that the United States will eventually lose its dollar as the reserve currency, two questions arise. One, what if the time that has been prophesized for thousands of years, the end, is upon the world in the very near future. After all, to consider President Trump as a possible candidate for the Antichrist, if that turned out to be true, if he really did turn out to be the Antichrist, then obviously time is very limited. The second question would be what would replace the US dollar as the reserve currency? Would it be a basket of currency, such as an SDR unit, perhaps with the United States still having an edge? Would one country really harbor much more control of the currency than another, at least at the same level that Americans can do it now? Questions, questions, questions...

There has been much written about the symbols on the United States currency, the Phoenix scenario, where out of the ashes of America the new world order will arise, as well as the United States being the new Atlantis (think Atlantic ocean). There has been talk of lay lines in Washington D.C. setup from its beginning as the center of the occult. There is even a famous church in New York City (Cathedral Church of Saint John the Divine) that has some stone carvings depicting Babylon as New York City, complete with mushroom clouds from nuclear explosions. So I ask the question, if the time was coming upon the world soon, if the United States was not the revived Roman empire, than which country would it be?

If one where to consider the possibility that the United States is the revived Roman empire, than one must consider the possibility that the Antichrist comes out of the United States. The Antichrist will have a powerful military at his disposal, of which the United States has the world's most powerful military. While Russia and the United States could utterly destroy each other, overall in terms of the amounts of investment into ships, carriers, weaponry, fighter jets and military technology, the United States dwarfs every other countries spending. The money is here and has been for quite some time. The Antichrist will control the revived Roman empire.

So why use President Trump as a perfect example to prove how the Antichrist could arise on the scene and the world, particularly that which calls itself Christian, would be unaware?

Well quite simply put, a warning needs to be given to those around the world who might be asking questions, trying to make sense of the nonstop changes taking place. For some, something doesn't seem right. For me, how could a warning not be given, one that reminds people to repent and accept Christ, to get back to being watching and ready, no matter who the Antichrist is or when the time of the end is? Thus, if the possibility remains, should not we as Christians be watchmen and as good soldiers of Jesus Christ, sound the warning trumpet if something could be amiss?

"When I say to the wicked, You shall die the death, and you give him no warning, nor speak to warn the wicked from his wicked way, to save his life, that same wicked man shall die in his iniquity; but his blood I will require at your hand. Yet, if you warn the wicked, and he does not turn from his wickedness, nor from his wicked way, he shall die in his iniquity; but you have delivered your soul. Again, when a righteous man turns from his righteousness and commits iniquity, and I lay a stumbling block before him, he shall die. Because you did not give him warning, he shall die in his sin, and his righteousness which he has done shall not be remembered; but his blood I will require at your hand. Nevertheless if you warn the righteous man that the righteous should not sin, and he does not sin, he shall live life because he took warning; and you have delivered your soul." Ezekiel 3:18-21

"You therefore endure hardship as a good soldier of Jesus Christ." 2nd Timothy 2:3

After all the end IS going to happen at some point. There will be a generation that will endure that. There will be a generation of Believers who will meet Christ in the air *(1 Thes. 4:17)*. There will be a generation that will have to contend with the Antichrist. There will be a generation that will go through the *"time of Jacob's trouble" (Jer. 30:7)*, better known as the Tribulation. So why use President Trump as the perfect example? Because he is and his followers are the perfect example of how a Strong Delusion sent by God could unfold. For those who are the most fascinated and strongest supporters of President Trump, likewise frequently make claims in their own personal lives as being Christians.

I've always been interested in end times events, never would I have thought myself to be one day writing about them. I looked and who is warning. As a Believer, through faith I am writing about this. I believe the Lord has instilled upon my heart to declare such things. Not to declare that President Trump is the Antichrist, but to point out how even if he was, the church is not watching and ready. When I first felt the necessity to write about such things, I thought, could not another *(Ex. 4:13)*?

For I must consider that if President Trump actually turned out to be unveiled as the Antichrist, would that not mean that he would be now??? For to be unveiled would simply mean to be able to be seen, but no one sensible seems to consider him a candidate, quite the opposite, they consider him to be God's chosen man. Yet, if he were to be, why should I want to steer up trouble by writing such things, though usually anything written is read only be a few.

In the past I have seen numerous websites about this or that person being the Antichrist or a candidate for the Antichrist, none of them ever settling with me as a real possibility. Perhaps some odd details, in my immaturity as a young Believer, that spiked a certain measure of interest, but never enough to actually ponder that that person could really be the Antichrist. I had read numerous things about President Obama potentially being the Antichrist, as there were MANY who said such things. Yet in my heart it never seemed right. With President Trump I started to notice some potential characteristics of the Antichrist seen in him, yet no one talking about it, at least not with even half a sense of properly using the Bible.

Even people whom I have read their political articles for years, these who claim to be Christians, have hopped on the Trump train. Whereas they had been very critical of everything before, pointing out legislation, history, etc., with President Trump he is essentially given a pass on anything he does. A brief example is how President Obama was heavily criticized sending more troops to Afghanistan, yet President Trump was praised for doing the same. This from the same people.

"You know what else they say about my people? The polls, they say I have the most loyal people. Did you ever see that? Where I could stand in the middle of Fifth Avenue and shoot somebody and I wouldn't lose any voters, okay?" - Donald Trump - Campaigning in 2016

Whether or not President Trump will turn out to be the Antichrist, I do not know. However, as I will point out, he makes the perfect example of proving just how far from the truth that what calls itself the church is nowadays. President Trump makes a perfect example of how those who call themselves christians, yet are not, seem to be deluded regarding him. He also makes the perfect example of how through genius schemes, he could ultimately rise to world power, though it would not be of his own power, but through the power of Satan. So we are going to be taking a look at some of the characteristics written about in The Antichrist chapter and comparing them to President Trump.

Not all of them will be looked at, there is simply too much vagueness with some of the biblical characteristics, as well as uncertainly. One thing is certain, eventually the Antichrist will rise on the scene, whoever he may be.

The Antichrist will have a Fierce Countenance and Understand Sinister Schemes

"In the finest traditions of our great democracy, we are rallying the noble nations of the world to build a new liberal order that prevents war and achieves greater prosperity for all," **- Mike Pompeo, United States Secretary of State**

The Antichrist will Rule the Entire World and the Economy

"The big uncertainty is the U.S.-China trade negotiation which is not really about trade, it's about a new world order," **Investec's Hendrik du Toit said at the World Economic Forum in Davos, Switzerland.**

In regards to China's foreign exchange currency policy, **President Trump responded,** *"I've been complaining about that for a long time, and I believe we will all eventually, and probably very much sooner than a lot of people understand or think, we will be on a level playing field, because that's the only way it's fair,"..."That's the only way you can fairly compete in trade and other things."*

"Bringing back the gold standard would be very hard to do, but boy, would it be wonderful. We'd have a standard on which to base our money." - **Donald Trump, Campaigning**

In regards to impeachment, *"If they actually did this the markets would crash. Do you think it was luck that got us to the best Stock Market and Economy in our history. It wasn't,"* - **President Trump, Tweet**

"I'll tell you what, if I ever got impeached, I think the market would crash. I think everybody would be very poor." - **President Trump**

"I am "the king of debt."That has been great for me as a businessman, but is bad for the country. I made a fortune off of debt, will fix U.S." - **Donald Trump, Campaigning, Tweet**

The Antichrist has Great Intelligence and is a Deceiver

"Sorry losers and haters, but my I.Q. is one of the highest -and you all know it! Please don't feel so stupid or insecure, it's not your fault," - **Donald Trump, Tweet, 2013**

"I know some of you may think I'm tough and harsh but actually I'm a very compassionate person (with a very high IQ) with strong common sense" - **Donald Trump, Tweet, 2013**

"I think that would qualify as not smart, but genius....and a very stable genius at that!" - **President Trump, Tweet**

The Antichrist shall honor the god of fortresses.

"And, by the way, I think I'm probably more hawkish than anybody. Anybody. Nobody is more hawkish than me. But I also like to use it in the right place. And, frankly, I like not using it at all." - **President Trump**

"We have the most powerful and well equipped military anywhere in the world, by far!" - **President Trump, Tweet**

"I think military is a very special thing." - **Donald Trump, Campaigning**

"There's nobody bigger or better at the military than I am." - **Donald Trump, Campaigning**

A Voice of a Man

"So on a set day Herod, arrayed in royal apparel, sat on his platform and gave an oration to them. And the people kept shouting, The voice of a god and not of a man! And immediately an angel of the Lord struck him, because he did not give glory to God. And he was eaten by worms and died." Acts 12:21-23

The other day I had gotten done finishing an article and publishing it online, as well as recording the radio shows for the upcoming days. I was pondering the current events in this world and thinking about how much different those in the patriotic circles, as well as the alternative media behave.

Prior to Donald Trump running for President of the United States, things hadn't changed much. After 9/11 a prepper movement began heavily in this country and there were people who were joining militias or planning for mutual aid in communities. There was a distrust of the Federal government and the word on the street was that martial law would eventually be declared.

As 2012 was closing in, the prepper movement, as well as the warnings hit their peak. My family had a year supply (for one person) of freeze dried food that we had purchased in 2011. In late 2013 we decided to sell it and had an older veteran stop over at our place in Whitefish, Montana, to pick it up.

This man described how he was part of a network where other patriots would do things, such as turn a home into a hospital, have food storages here and there, as well as communications, etc. He wasn't alone, he wasn't crazy, he simply believed, as many did, that eventually the Federal government was going to turn on the people and preparing for such things just made sense.

Now we have a country of conspiracy theorists, of which I would agree with much of that, though I would call it conspiracy facts in many cases. Yet the mass of people have bought into the fake news, fake media, etc. They no longer believe the 'lies' that are told on the media, rather they are following the man, President Trump. For many, what President Trump says is the truth, irregardless of what others say.

This is not to say that President Trump is lying about the media, it has been controlled by a handful of people, a sort of oligopoly that is fed by the United States ministry of 'truth'. The media shouldn't have been trusted twenty years ago, let alone today. The problem lies with those who had always been saying that the media was controlled.

For the most part, all of the main alternative media talking heads are no longer discussing the Federal government's plans for a martial law scenario. In fact, everything is focused on the fact that there is now a man in the Whitehouse who is cleaning it up. 'One of us' is now in control of the country and he is fighting the deep state, new world order, whatever you might call it, to whatever level you believe that the conspiracy goes.

Where there were people like Ron Paul (who is not an avid Trump supporter) warning us about how a wall built on the southern border could be used to keep us in, there are now only those telling us that the wall built is for the intentions stated and they mention no possibility of anything else.

They are quick to point out the health hazards of a 5G network being rapidly deployed across the United States, but they refuse to acknowledge or mention the military implications for potential real-time warfare against the American public. Imagine martial law plugged into the 5G network! Try to get away from that technology of real time updates!

Where war with Afghanistan and Middle Eastern countries was always part of the conspiracy of the petro-dollar, the dreams of Dick Cheney and the military industrial complex, now it is either necessary or with President Trump openly admitting it is about the oil, this is alright. Well, then they should have kept their mouth shut all along, if the world reserve currency, the US dollar is dependent on control of the oil and the wars, as well as operations that go along with it, then why was it ever a problem? Do really the ends justify the means? I guess in our so-called 'christian' nation it is alright to behave like that.

"Woe to those who draw iniquity with cords of vanity, and sin with cart ropes; who say, Let Him hurry and hasten His work, so that we may see it; and let the purpose of the Holy One of Israel draw near and come, so that we may know it! Woe to those who call evil good and good evil; who put darkness for light and light for darkness; who put bitter for sweet and sweet for bitter! Woe to those who are wise in their own eyes, and understanding in their own sight! Woe to those mighty to drink wine, and men of strength to mix strong drink; who justify the wicked for a bribe, and take away justice from the righteous!" Isaiah 5:18-23

Even President Obama eventually put a stop to militarizing the police stations across the United States, due to a huge outcry over civil rights and potential police abuse. Yet with the stroke of a pen and with section 1033 fully operational, the hardening of the police forces across the United States with sophisticated weaponry and military vehicles at a record level, President Trump revamped and accelerated the program. This same program was always talked about by the alternative media of proof that the Federal government was getting ready for martial law. Now? Not even a peep!

Did FEMA cancel all of the contracts to have instant 72 hour operational tent cities? Did our government finally decide that it can not handle the American people in an operation against the 'hold outs'? Or did the original conspiracy theorist decide that martial law was never a possibility? Well President Trump changed all of that!

Certainly when he passed an executive order (EO) that seems to allow for military tribunals, martial law, in a fallen society, that was not the real purpose, right? After all the same talking heads told of how that EO was really for the deep state. President Trump, as I have heard time and time again, and seen numerous articles about, is planning on using that to get rid of the deep state. According to these people, President Trump will have to temporarily suspend the Constitution, declare martial law and have military tribunals for the Pelosi's, Obama's, Clinton's, etc., and their helpers.

Time and time again, things that were once believed, once warned about, are now turned upside down. The solution is always the same, irregardless if it is from the evangelicals or the alternative media or even just the republican party...trust in President Trump, he will take care of it.

Just as the alternative media ignores the SAME warning signs that are going on, the ones they used to scream about for people to wake up, so too the evangelicals overlook President Trump's doctrines of prosperity, sex (thinking of the Playboy cover Trump was featured on), greed, materialism and pride. They simply say to trust in him, he is a man chosen by God. Really?

Even the republican party has been overcome by the 'if you can't beat them, join them' philosophy. Their constituents demand support for President Trump, therefore their own jobs are on the line. Well you say, where is your proof, how come you don't join us?

I was thinking about these things and decided to do some deeper research, trying to figure out what was currently being said from the alternative media, as well as just the 'average joe' with their blogs, websites, etc. I also looked at what the mainstream media was saying.

I pondered these things and was also looking at how very popular pastors and religious leaders in this country were advocating for President Trump, speaking against the impeachment and calling him God's chosen man. What I eventually ran across was something that I hadn't heard, hadn't seen.

I knew there was a bunch of prominent rabbis who state that President Trump is either the messiah or else he is helping to usher in the messiah. I understand that this messiah that the religious Jews of Israel are looking for, will ultimately be the Antichrist. What I didn't original know, but my best friend managed to find out, is that the rabbis look to the messiah, not as God incarnate, but rather as a political leader who will place Israel back into their supposed rightful place in time.

Israel does not understand *"the time of Jacob's trouble" (Jer. 30:7)*, and neither does the church. Both do not know and in doing so they are fulfilling the prophecies about such a time that the Bible talks about. However, I continued to ponder these things and then, if it wasn't bad enough that President Trump was compared to Jesus Christ and His crucifixion, matters got worse.

President Trump retweeted a video of a man talking about how Israel views him, that he was like the 'second coming of God' or the 'king of Israel'. In another video, when talking about the tariffs with China, President Trump looks up to the sky, as if looking towards Heaven, and states that he 'is the chosen one'. With the later President Trump claims it is sarcasm, yet with the first that President Trump retweeted, he simply added the word "wow!" to his retweet.

When Jesus was accused of the same thing:

"And as He was now drawing near the descent of the Mount of Olives, the whole multitude of the disciples began to rejoice and praise God with a loud voice for all the mighty works they had seen, saying: Blessed is the King who comes in the name of the Lord! Peace in Heaven and glory in the highest! And some of the Pharisees called to Him from the crowd, Teacher, rebuke Your disciples. But He answered and said to them, I tell you that if these should keep silent, the stones would immediately cry out." Luke 19:37-40

Jesus rightfully so, did not dispute with what men were saying about Him, but rather stated that if they kept silent the stones would immediately cry out. He is the Son of God *(John 3:16, etc.)*, He is God *(John 10:30)*. Yet President Trump simply retweeted it, sucking it all in, as Herod had done. If that didn't please God back then, certainly it is not pleasing to our Creator now.

President Trump is the voice of a man, not of a god. He should stop his followers from comparing himself to Jesus Christ, Elijah, Moses or the King of Israel, of which Christ is the King *(Zec. 9:9)*! When you consider what was stated in the previous chapters in retrospect to what is being written here, truly we live in a time of utter ignorance of the Bible, we are certainly in the last days.

Once again I do not know the future, I do not know whether President Trump will simply be President of the United States or something more, but what I do know is there has never been a President in history that has been compared to Jesus, Moses or Elijah, let alone called the King of Israel or suggesting that he is like the Second Coming. We live in very ignorant and apostate times.

"And they shall wander from sea to sea, and from the north even to the east; they shall roam to and fro to seek the Word of Jehovah, and they shall not find it." Amos 8:11

Amen!

His Glorious Appearing

"For the grace of God that brings salvation has appeared to all men, teaching us that, denying ungodliness and worldly lusts, we should live with sound mind, righteously, and godly in the present age, looking for the blessed hope and glorious appearing of our great God and Savior Jesus Christ, who gave Himself for us, that He might redeem us from all lawlessness and purify a people for His own possession, zealous unto good works." Titus 2:11-14

There has been much debate regarding the Rapture, which could be better termed His Glorious Appearing. There are even many pastors who sit on the fence, not knowing whether or not His Glorious Appearing is pre-tribulation or post-tribulation. Yet the Bible is quite clear and common sense should prevail that the Rapture will happen prior to the *"time of Jacob's trouble" (Jer. 30:7)*, better known as the Tribulation.

The purpose in this chapter is not to just provide the evidence of the pre-trib Rapture being a sound doctrine, but also to provide needed information for those souls who will read such things, after having been Left Behind. For those whom God allows to be deluded by the Strong Delusion, what can be done? There opportunity for Salvation is prior to the Rapture and if they are those whom God is allowing to believe the lie *(2 Thes. 2:11)*, after the Rapture, then their fate is sealed *(Rev. 20:15)*.

Consider the following verses:

"And none of the wicked shall understand, but the wise shall understand." Daniel 12:10b

"At that time Jesus answered and said, I thank You, Father, Lord of Heaven and earth, that You have hidden these things from the wise and intelligent, and have revealed them to babes." Matthew 11:25

"And He said, To you it has been given to know the mysteries of the kingdom of God, but to the rest in parables, that seeing they may not see, and hearing they may not understand." Luke 8:10

What many churches fail to recognize is that the Lord Jesus comes back twice. Though once is His Glorious Appearing, where He does not set foot upon the earth, the other is His Second Coming. The Bible is quite clear as distinguishing two separate events, for those who may see and hear.

"I charge you therefore before God and the Lord Jesus Christ, who will judge the living and the dead at <u>His appearing and His kingdom</u>:" 2nd Timothy 4:1

His Glorious Appearing is the end of the Church age, the Church is Raptured. His Second Coming is His revealing Himself to Israel, it is all about God's chosen people. While the world will be judged, the *"time of Jacob's trouble" (Jer. 30:7)* is about Israel. Oftentimes the two of these get mixed up and create all sort of false doctrines and movements. Let me try to clear some of the confusion up regarding these two separate events.

Starting with the end of the Church age and those who are truly Saved, let's take a look at His Glorious Appearing, better known as the Rapture, as to why the Church or those who are Saved cannot be here during the Tribulation. Then let's take a look at some clear distinctions that what people assume to be verses that point to a post-trib are clearly discussing His Second Coming, which is the revelation of Jesus Christ *(Lk. 17:30, 1 Pet. 1:13, Rev. 1:1)* to the Jewish people, two separate events.

There are some scoffers who say that those who believe in the pre-trib Rapture are not willing to suffer through the Tribulation. That as Jesus suffered on the Cross, so too must all of the Church suffer. Well the Church has been suffering for 2,000 years.

"These things I have spoken to you, that in Me you may have peace. In the world you have affliction; but be of good courage, I have overcome the world." John 16:33

..." strengthening the souls of the disciples, exhorting them to continue in the faith, and that we must enter the kingdom of God through many afflictions." Acts 14:22

So the clear cut argument that is given in the United States is that Believers do not suffer, perhaps some name calling, etc. Yet, if one actually stands for what the Bible teaches and does not shy away from living separated from the world, there is affliction.

"Therefore, Come out from among them and be separate, says the Lord. Do not touch what is unclean, and I will receive you." 2nd Corinthians 6:17

I dare say that a majority of these who retort such things to true Believers, those who wrongly believe in the post-trib Rapture are not Saved themselves. So why should they have affliction preaching a different Jesus *(2 Cor. 11:4)* and doctrines of demons *(1 Tim. 4:1)*? One should not look at solely the United States of America as an example of harsh affliction that the true Saints throughout the ages have experienced on behalf of Christ.

For the United States was setup as a country for religious freedom, unlike most of the world. There was a reason that our forefathers came here. To focus solely on the United States is to be blind to the facts of history regarding the true Church.

The Bible is quite clear that Hades will not prevail against the Church, but we find that the saints during the *"time of Jacob's trouble" (Jer. 30:7)* are prevailed against.

"And I also say to you that you are Peter, and on this Rock I will build My church, and the gates of Hades shall not prevail against It." Matthew 16:18

"And it was granted to him to make war with the saints and to overcome them. And authority was given him over every tribe, tongue, and nation." Revelation 13:7

"After these things I looked, and behold, a great multitude which no one was able to number, of all nations, tribes, peoples, and tongues, standing before the throne and before the Lamb, clothed with white robes, with palm branches in their hands, and crying out with a loud voice, saying, Salvation belongs to our God who sits on the throne, and to the Lamb!" Revelation 7:9-10

"Then one of the elders answered, saying to me, Who are these arrayed in white robes, and where did they come from? And I said to him, Sir, you know. So he said to me, These are the ones coming out of great affliction, and have washed their robes and made them white in the blood of the Lamb. Therefore they are before the throne of God, and serve Him day and night in His temple. And He who sits on the throne will spread His tabernacle over them. They shall neither hunger anymore nor thirst anymore; the sun shall not fall on them, nor any burning heat; for the Lamb who is in the midst of the throne will shepherd them and lead them to living fountains of waters. And God will wipe away every tear from their eyes." Revelation 7:13-17

"And I saw thrones, and they sat on them, and judgment was committed to them; and I saw the souls of those who had been beheaded for their witness to Jesus and for the Word of God, who had not done homage to the beast or his image, and had not received his mark on their foreheads or on their hands. And they lived and reigned with Christ for a thousand years." Revelation 20:4

So who would be left to be Raptured at the end of the Tribulation? For those who are truly Christians, who have repented and by faith believed into Jesus Christ as their Savior *(Ro. 8:10-13, Ac. 17:30-31, Eph. 2:8-10)*, are with the Lord *(1 Th. 4:17)*. For during the Tribulation the Antichrist is allowed to overcome the post-Church age saints, that is those who receive Salvation during the *"time of Jacob's trouble" (Jer. 30:7)*.

Quite obvious is also the fact that when the Second Coming happens, when Jesus Christ sets His feet upon the Mount of Olives *(Zec. 14:4)*, the saints are coming with Him. How can they be coming back with Him, if they are still here?

"And you shall flee to the valley of My mountains, for the valley of the mountains shall reach to Azal. And you shall flee as you fled before the earthquake in the days of Uzziah, king of Judah. And Jehovah my God shall come, and all the saints with You." Zechariah 14:5

..."so that He may establish your hearts blameless in holiness before our God and Father at the coming of our Lord Jesus Christ with all His saints." 1st Thessalonians 3:13

Though there is still discussions and debates about these things, nowadays churches simply aren't teaching these things. They either cannot make up their mind, allow different opinions are have moved along unto other things. The Bible prophesized this as well.

"Beloved, I now write to you this second epistle (in both of which I stir up your pure minds by way of reminder), that you may remember the words which were spoken before by the holy prophets, and the commandment of us, the apostles of the Lord and Savior, knowing this first: that scoffers will come in the last days, walking according to their own lusts, and saying, Where is the promise of His coming? For since the fathers fell asleep, all things continue as they were since the beginning of creation." 2nd Peter 3:1-4

The Bible is quite clear about there being a Rapture, which should aptly be called His Glorious Appearing, but Rapture is also quite acceptable.

"For if we believe that Jesus died and rose again, even so God will bring with Him those who sleep in Jesus. For this we say to you by the Word of the Lord, that we who are alive and remain until the coming of the Lord will by no means precede those who are asleep. For the Lord Himself will descend from Heaven with a shouted *command, with the voice of the archangel, and with the trumpet of God. And the dead in Christ will rise first. Then we who are alive and remain shall be caught up together* at the same time *with them in the clouds to meet the Lord in the air. And thus we shall always be with the Lord. Therefore encourage one another with these words."* 1st Thessalonians 4:14-18

"Behold, I tell you a mystery: We shall not all sleep, but we shall all be changed; in a moment, in the twinkling of an eye, at the last trumpet. For the trumpet will sound, and the dead will be raised incorruptible, and we shall be changed." 1st Corinthians 15:51-52

"And if I go and prepare a place for you, I will come again and receive you to Myself; that where I am, there you may be also." John 14:3

The argument of the Rapture being a silent thing should not be. For quite clearly the Lord Himself will descend from Heaven with a -shouted- command and also the trumpet will sound. For those scoffers, do not necessarily think that you have a foolproof argument that the trumpet is the same as the seventh trumpet in Revelation, for you do not. One must look at the Holy Scriptures as a whole, not pick and chose which verses fit the theories that one wants to propagate upon the masses.

The Bible is quite clear that the Church, though appointed through the afflictions, persecutions and tribulations of this life, are not appointed to wrath.

...*"and to wait for His Son from Heaven, whom He raised from the dead, even Jesus who delivers us from the coming wrath."* 1st Thessalonians 1:10

"For God did not appoint us to wrath, but to obtain salvation through our Lord Jesus Christ, who died for us, that whether we watch or sleep, we should live together with Him." 1st Thessalonians 5:9-10

"There is no fear in love; but perfect love casts out fear, because fear involves punishment. But he who fears has not been made complete in love." 1st John 4:18

Consider this verse in comparison of this:

"And the kings of the earth, the great men, the rich men, the commanders, the mighty men, every slave and every free man, hid themselves in the caves and in the rocks of the mountains, and said to the mountains and rocks, Fall on us and hide us from the face of Him who sits on the throne and from the wrath of the Lamb! For the great day of His wrath has come, and who is able to stand?" Revelation 6:15-17

Also...

"Because you have kept the Word of My perseverance, I also will keep you from the hour of trial which shall come upon the whole world, to test those who dwell on the earth." Revelation 3:10

"After these things I looked, and behold, a door having been opened in Heaven. And the first voice which I heard was like a trumpet speaking with me, saying, Come up here, and I will show you things which must take place after these things." Revelation 4:1

There are some passages of the Bible that teach clearly about the Rapture, but ALSO about the Second Coming. This is often a problem with those who hold the post-trib false viewpoint, they fail to recognize these things.

"3 Now as He sat on the Mount of Olives, the disciples came to Him privately, saying, Tell us, when will these things be? And what will be the sign of Your coming, and of the end of the age?
4 And Jesus answered and said to them: Take heed that no one leads you astray.
5 For many will come in My name, saying, I am the Christ, and will lead many astray.
6 And you will hear of wars and rumors of wars. See that you are not troubled; for all these things must come to pass, but the end is not yet.
7 For nation will rise against nation, and kingdom against kingdom. And there will be famines, pestilences, and earthquakes in various places.
8 All these are the beginning of travail.
9 Then they will deliver you up to affliction and kill you, and you will be hated by all nations because of My name.
10 And then many will be offended, will betray one another, and will hate one another.
11 And many false prophets will rise up and lead many astray.
12 And because lawlessness will abound, the love of many will grow cold.
13 But he who endures to the end shall be kept safe.
14 And this gospel of the kingdom will be preached in all the world as a testimony to all the nations, and then the end will come.
15 Therefore when you see the abomination of desolation, spoken of by Daniel the prophet, standing in the holy place (whoever reads, let him understand),
16 then let those who are in Judea flee into the mountains.
17 Let him who is on the housetop not go down to take anything out of his house.
18 And let him who is in the field not go back to get his clothes.

19 But woe to those who are pregnant and to those who are nursing babies in those days!
20 And pray that your flight may not be in winter or on the Sabbath.
21 For then there will be great affliction, such as has not been since the beginning of the world until this time, no, nor ever shall be.
22 And unless those days were shortened, no flesh would be kept safe alive; *but for the elect's sake those days will be shortened.*
23 Then if anyone says to you, Look, here is the Christ; or, There; do not believe it.
24 For false christs and false prophets will arise and show great signs and wonders to lead astray, if possible, even the elect.
25 Behold, I have told you beforehand.
26 Therefore if they say to you, Behold, He is in the desert, do not go out; or, Behold, He is in the inner rooms, do not believe it.
27 For as the lightning comes out of the east and flashes to the west, so also will the coming of the Son of Man be.
28 For wherever the carcass is, there the eagles will be gathered together.
29 And immediately after the affliction of those days the sun will be darkened, and the moon will not give its light; the stars will fall from heaven, and the powers of the heavens will be shaken.
30 And then the sign of the Son of Man will appear in the heavens, and then all the tribes of the earth will wail, and they will see the Son of Man coming on the clouds of heaven with power and great glory.
31 And He will send His angels with a great sound of a trumpet, and they will gather together His elect from the four winds, from one end of heaven to the other.
32 Now learn this parable from the fig tree: When its branch has already become tender and puts forth leaves, you know that summer is near.
33 So you also, when you see all these things, know that it is near, at the doors.
34 Truly, I say to you, this generation will by no means pass away till all these things are fulfilled.
35 Heaven and earth will pass away, but My Words will by no means pass away.
36 But of that day and hour no one knows, not even the angels of Heaven, but My Father only.
37 But as the days of Noah were, so also will the coming of the Son of Man be.
38 For as in the days before the flood, they were eating and drinking, marrying and giving in marriage, until the day that Noah entered into the ark,
39 and did not realize until the flood came and took them all away, so also will the coming of the Son of Man be.
40 Then two will be in the field: one is taken and the other is left.
41 Two will be grinding at the mill: one is taken and the other is left.
42 Watch therefore, for you do not know what hour your Lord comes.
43 But know this, that if the master of the house had known what hour the thief comes, he would have watched and not allowed his house to be dug through.
44 Therefore you also be ready, for the Son of Man comes at an hour you do not expect.
45 Who then is a faithful and wise servant, whom his master made administrator over his household, to give them food in due season?
46 Blessed is that servant whom his master, when he comes, will find so doing.
47 Truly, I say to you that he will appoint him as *administrator over all his possessions.*

48 But if that wicked servant says in his heart, My master delays his coming,
49 and begins to beat his fellow servants, and to eat and drink with the drunkards,
50 the master of that servant will come on a day when he is not expecting him and in an hour he does not know,
51 and will cut him in two and appoint him his portion with the hypocrites. There shall be weeping and gnashing of teeth." Matthew 24:3-51

"And He said to the disciples, The days will come when you will desire to see one of the days of the Son of Man, and you will not see it.
23 And they will say to you, Look here; or, Look there. Do not go away nor follow.
24 For as the lightning that flashes out of one part under the heavens, shines to the other part under the heavens, so also the Son of Man will be in His day.
25 But first He must suffer many things and be rejected from this generation.
26 And as it was in the days of Noah, so it will be also in the days of the Son of Man:
27 They ate, they drank, they married wives, they were given in marriage, until the day that Noah entered into the ark, and the flood came and destroyed them all.
28 Likewise as it was also in the days of Lot: They ate, they drank, they bought, they sold, they planted, they built;
29 but on the day that Lot went out of Sodom it rained fire and brimstone from heaven and destroyed them all.
30 Even in the same way will it be in the day when the Son of Man is revealed.
31 In that day, he who will be on the housetop, and his goods are in the house, let him not come down to take them away. And likewise the one who is in the field, let him not return back.
32 Remember Lot's wife.
33 Whoever seeks to save his life will lose it, and whoever loses his life will preserve it.
34 I tell you, in that night there will be two in one bed: the one will be taken and the other will be left.
35 Two will be grinding together: the one will be taken and the other left.
36 Two will be in the field: the one will be taken and the other left.
37 And they answered and said to Him, Where, Lord? And He said to them, Wherever the body is, there the eagles will be gathered together." Luke 17:22-37

Clearly when two are together and one is taken, the other left, this is teaching about the Rapture. An interesting thing is that you will see that two are in a bed, as well as two are working. When the Rapture happens, for some in the world it will be nighttime, for others it will be daytime.

In Matthew 24:42 clearly it states 'your Lord' which is talking about Christians, but in Matthew 24:31 it speaks of Christ gathering His elect. The Church has never been termed the elect, that is clearly Israel.

"For Jacob My servant's sake, and Israel My elect, I have even proclaimed your name; I have entitled you, though you have not known Me." Isaiah 45:4

Israel will not be Raptured, except those individuals who are truly Saved, as they are yet in unbelief and will not believe until the Second Coming.

"In that day Jehovah shall defend the inhabitants of Jerusalem. And he who is feeble among them in that day shall be *like David, and the house of David* shall be *like God, like the Angel of Jehovah before them. And it shall be in that day,* that *I will seek to destroy all the nations that come against Jerusalem. And I will pour on the house of David, and on the inhabitants of Jerusalem, the Spirit of grace and supplication. And they shall look on Me whom they have pierced; and they shall mourn for Him, as one mourns for an only* son, *and* they *shall be bitter over Him, like the bitterness over the firstborn." Zechariah 12:8-10*

For those scoffers who declare that there will be a Rapture of the evil ones, you know who you are, then pay attention and take heed!

"And as for you, son of man, thus says the Lord Jehovah, Speak to every sort of bird and to every beast of the field: Assemble yourselves and come; gather together from all sides to My sacrifice which I am sacrificing for you, a great sacrifice on the mountains of Israel, that you may eat flesh and drink blood. You shall eat the flesh of the mighty, drink the blood of the rulers of the earth, of rams and lambs, of goats and bulls, all of them fatlings of Bashan. You shall eat fat till you are full, and drink blood till you are drunk, at My sacrifice which I have sacrificed for you. You shall be filled at My table with horses and riders, with mighty men and with all the men of war, says the Lord Jehovah. And I will set My glory among the nations; all the nations shall see My judgments which I have executed, and My hand which I have laid on them. Thus the house of Israel shall know that I am Jehovah their God from that day forward. And the nations shall know that the house of Israel went into captivity for their iniquity; because they were unfaithful to Me, therefore I hid My face from them. I gave them into the hand of their enemies, and they all fell by the sword. According to their uncleanness and according to their transgressions I have dealt with them, and hidden My face from them. Therefore thus says the Lord Jehovah: Now I will bring back the captives of Jacob, and have mercy on the whole house of Israel; and I will be jealous for My holy name; after they have borne their shame, and all their treachery in which they were unfaithful to Me, when they dwelt safely in their own land and no one made them afraid. When I have brought them back from the peoples and gathered them out of the lands of their enemies, and I am sanctified in them in the eyes of many nations, then they shall know that I am Jehovah their God, who sent them into captivity among the nations, but also brought them back to their own land, and left none of them there. And I will not hide My face from them anymore; for I have poured out My Spirit on the house of Israel, declares the Lord Jehovah." Ezekiel 39:17-29

"And I saw an angel standing in the sun; and he cried with a loud voice, saying to all the birds that fly in the midst of the heavens, Come and gather together for the supper of the great God, that you may eat the flesh of kings, the flesh of commanders, the flesh of mighty men, the flesh of horses and of those who sit on them, and the flesh of all people, free and slave, both small and great. And I saw the beast, the kings of the earth, and

their armies, gathered together to make war against Him who sat on the horse and against His army. And the beast was captured, and with him the false prophet who worked signs in his presence, by which he led astray those who received the mark of the beast and those who did homage to his image. These two were cast alive into the Lake of Fire burning with brimstone. And the rest were killed with the sword which proceeded out of the mouth of Him who sat on the horse. And all the birds were filled with their flesh." Revelation 19:17-21

Do not confuse the Second Coming of Christ to His Glorious Appearing. For Jesus appears at the Rapture, but He does not set His feet upon the earth. His Second Coming is a distinctive event.

"And I saw Heaven opened, and behold, a white horse. And He who sat on him was called Faithful and True, and in righteousness He judges and makes war." Revelation 19:11

"Behold, the day of Jehovah comes, and your spoils shall be divided in your midst. For I will gather all the nations to battle against Jerusalem. And the city shall be captured, and the houses plundered, and the women ravished. And half the city shall go into captivity and the rest of the people shall not be cut off from the city. And Jehovah shall go forth and fight against those nations, like the day He fought in the day of battle. And His feet shall stand in that day on the Mount of Olives, which is before Jerusalem on the east; and the Mount of Olives shall split in two, from the east even to the west, a very great valley. And half of the mountain shall move toward the north, and half of it toward the south. And you shall flee to the valley of My mountains, for the valley of the mountains shall reach to Azal. And you shall flee as you fled before the earthquake in the days of Uzziah, king of Judah. And Jehovah my God shall come, and all the saints with You. And it will come to pass in that day, that there shall not be light; the great lights will shrink. And it will be one day which shall be known to Jehovah; not day and not night, but it will happen, that there will be light at evening time. And it shall be in that day, that living waters shall go out from Jerusalem, half of them toward the eastern sea, and half of them toward the western sea; in summer and in winter it shall be. And Jehovah shall be King over all the earth. In that day there shall be one Jehovah, and His name one. All the land shall be changed into a plain from Geba to Rimmon south of Jerusalem. And it shall rise and dwell in its place, from Benjamin's Gate to the place of the First Gate, to the Corner Gate, and from the Tower of Hananeel to the king's winepresses. And they shall live in it. And there shall never again be utter destruction, but Jerusalem shall dwell safely. And this shall be the plague with which Jehovah will strike all the people who have fought against Jerusalem: Their flesh shall rot away while they stand on their feet, and their eyes will rot away in their sockets, and their tongues shall rot away in their mouths. And it shall happen in that day, that a great confusion from Jehovah shall be among them; and they shall each one lay hold of his neighbor, and his hand shall rise up against the hand of his neighbor." Zechariah 14:1-13

In Matthew 24:30 the *"sign of the Son of Man will appear in the heavens, and then all the tribes of the earth will wail"*. Clearly no one knows the day, nor the hour *(Matt. 24:36)*.

There will be signs of Christ's imminent Second Coming, as there are many prophecies that will be fulfilled. If true Believers were here during that time we could simply count from the "abomination", until the Lord returns.

"And from the time the regular sacrifice *shall be taken away, and the abomination that causes horror* is *set up,* there shall be *one thousand, two hundred and ninety days."* Daniel 12:11

or...

"And I heard the man clothed in linen, who was *on the waters of the river, when he held up his right and his left* hand *to the heavens and swore by Him who lives forever, that it* shall be *for a time, times, and a half. And when they have made an end of scattering the power of the holy people, all these* things *shall be finished."* Daniel 12:7

or

"Then the woman fled into the wilderness, where she has a place prepared by God, that they should feed her there one thousand two hundred and sixty days." Revelation 12:6

or

"But the woman was given two wings of a great eagle, that she might fly into the wilderness to her place, where she is nourished for a time and times and half a time, from the presence of the serpent." Revelation 12:14

or

"And he was given a mouth speaking great things and blasphemies, and he was given authority to continue for forty-two months." Revelation 13:5

Clearly it would be contrary that no one would know the day nor the hour, verses being able to count the days from the time that the abomination of desolation is setup by the Antichrist. One could simply count out the days and know for sure when Jesus was coming.

There used to be a time when the Churches in this country believed what the Bible says. Just as many churches now believe that homosexuality, gay marriage, even transgenderism is acceptable, so too their Rapture doctrine, if they have one, is far from what the Word of God teaches.

The apostasy is in full bloom and things are not going to get any better. There are no more warning signs, nothing that needs to happen, the Rapture is imminent and could happen at any moment. When that will be is not known, but until then, we who are Believers need to be watching and ready.

"Watch therefore, and pray always that you may be counted worthy to escape all these things that will come to pass, and to stand before the Son of Man." Luke 21:36

Dear reader, there are a lot of scary things that will happen during the *"time of Jacob's trouble" (Jer. 30:7)*. So what happens if you didn't know, if you were deceived and because you were not truly Saved, even if you thought you were, you were Left Behind?

Even though God sends a Strong Delusion, that Strong Delusion is for those who made a willful choice to deny God, for those who refused to repent and believe the Gospel. There are countless people who have made professions of faith, without even really understanding the Gospel.

I suspect that if you are reading such a thing as this and pondering what to do now, that you are not part of those whom God is allowing to believe the lie. Salvation is simple for those who are Left Behind. There won't be much time to learn in depth doctrine, in fact finding a Bible might be nearly impossible *(Am. 8:11)*, especially a good translation.

Call upon the Lord and do not be like the world who refuse to repent *(Rev. 9:20-21, 16:11)*. Rather put your trust in your Creator, even unto death. For what will you give in exchange for your soul? You only have one chance in this life, and this is your one chance! I beg of you to yield to God and let Him take care of the rest.

"And it shall be, that whoever shall call on the name of Jehovah shall escape. For in Mount Zion and in Jerusalem shall be deliverance, as Jehovah has said, and among the survivors whom Jehovah shall call." Joel 2:32

"But what does it say? The Word is near you, in your mouth and in your heart (that is, the Word of Faith which we preach): that if you confess with your mouth the Lord Jesus and believe in your heart that God has raised Him from the dead, you will be saved. For with the heart one believes unto righteousness, and with the mouth confession is made unto salvation. For the Scripture says, Everyone believing on Him will not be put to shame. For there is no distinction between Jew and Greek, for the same Lord over all is rich toward all who call upon Him. For everyone, whoever calls on the name of the Lord shall be saved." Romans 10:8-13

"For this God is our God forever and ever; He will be our guide even unto death." Psalms 48:14

"And when He had called the people to Himself, with His disciples also, He said to them, Whoever desires to come after Me, let him deny himself, and take up his cross, and follow Me. For whoever desires to save his life will lose it, but whoever loses his life for My sake and the gospel's will save it. For what will it profit a man if he gains the whole world, and loses his own soul? Or what will a man give in exchange for his soul? For whoever is ashamed of Me and My words in this adulterous and sinful generation, of him the Son of Man also will be ashamed when He comes in the glory of His Father with the holy angels." Mark 8:34-38

"And as it is appointed for men to die once, and after this the judgment, so Christ was offered once to bear the sins of many. To those who eagerly wait for Him He will appear a second time, without sin, unto salvation." Hebrews 9:27-28

"Trust in Jehovah with all your heart, and lean not unto your own understanding. In all your ways acknowledge Him, and He shall direct your paths. Do not be wise in your own eyes; fear Jehovah and depart from evil. It shall be healing to your navel and refreshment to your bones." Proverbs 3:5-8

Amen!

The End is Near

"Him we preach, warning every man and teaching every man in all wisdom, that we may present every man complete in Christ Jesus." Colossians 1:28

"And I will bring distress upon men, and they shall walk like the blind, because they have sinned against Jehovah. And their blood shall be poured out as dust, and their flesh like dung." Zephaniah 1:17

What happened to those who used to hold up signs in our big cities declaring that 'the end is near'? Movies on occasion used to add such things, often a ridicule to those who would be presumed to be mentally unstable. Yet has not the Word of God proclaimed that the end will eventually come?

"And this gospel of the kingdom will be preached in all the world as a testimony to all the nations, and then the end will come. " Matthew 24:14

Well there are two 'ends' to be precise. There is the Rapture, which is the end of the Church age and then there is the end, which is the end of the *"time of Jacob's trouble" (Jer. 30:7)*, better known as the Tribulation. Even then we could argue the Millennial reign, etc., but our job as Believers is the warn people to repent and believe the Gospel.

...*"testifying both to Jews, and also to Greeks, repentance toward God and faith toward our Lord Jesus Christ." Acts 20:21*

"Truly, these times of ignorance God overlooked, but now commands all men everywhere to repent, because He has established a day on which He will judge the world in righteousness by the Man whom He has appointed. He has given assurance of this to everyone by raising Him from the dead." Acts 17:30-31

So here we are, in what may very well be the final last days prior to the end and very few people contemplate it. Even the churches, whom should be warning men have refused to preach repentance, refused to purify themselves and are by and large apostate. However, these simple facts even provide further evidence that the end is near.

"But know this, that in the last days perilous times will come: For men will be lovers of themselves, lovers of money, boasters, proud, blasphemers, disobedient to parents, unthankful, unholy, without natural affection, unyielding, slanderers, without self-control, savage, despisers of good, traitors, headstrong, haughty, lovers of pleasure rather than lovers of God, having a form of godliness but denying its power. And from such people turn away. For of this sort are those who creep into households and make captives of gullible women loaded down with sins, led away by various lusts, always learning, but never able to come to the full true knowledge of the truth. But as Jannes and Jambres opposed Moses, so do these also oppose the truth: men of corrupt minds, reprobate concerning the faith; but they will progress no further, for their folly will be manifest to all, as theirs also was." 2nd Timothy 3:1-9

"Beloved, I now write to you this second epistle (in both of which I stir up your pure minds by way of reminder), that you may remember the words which were spoken before by the holy prophets, and the commandment of us, the apostles of the Lord and Savior, knowing this first: that scoffers will come in the last days, walking according to their own lusts, and saying, Where is the promise of His coming? For since the fathers fell asleep, all things continue as they were since the beginning of creation." 2nd Peter 3:1-4

"And to the angel of the church of the Laodiceans write, These things says the Amen, the Faithful and True Witness, the Beginning of the creation of God: I know your works, that you are neither cold nor hot. I would that you were cold or hot. So then, because you are lukewarm, and neither cold nor hot, I will vomit you out of My mouth. Because you say, I am rich, have become wealthy, and have need of nothing; and do not know that you are wretched and miserable and poor and blind and naked; I counsel you to buy from Me gold refined in the fire, that you may be rich; and white garments, that you may be clothed, that the shame of your nakedness may not be revealed; and anoint your eyes with eye salve, that you may see. As many as I love, I rebuke and chasten. Therefore be zealous and repent. Behold, I stand at the door and knock. If anyone hears My voice and opens the door, I will come in to him and dine with him, and he with Me. To him who overcomes I will grant to sit with Me on My throne, as I also overcame and sat down with My Father on His throne. He who has an ear, let him hear what the Spirit says to the churches." Revelation 3:14-22

For if preachers where still preaching about watching and being ready for the Rapture, if they were still warning men about the coming Tribulation, if they were still pointing out to the lost that eventually the Antichrist would be unveiled (after the Rapture) and that he would have a peace deal with Israel, then perhaps not many who listened would be caught off guard, but they would be able to repent and by faith believe into Jesus Christ.

Men could ponder these things, they could examine themselves *(2 Cor. 13:5)*, they could truly seek the Most High, they could become Saved. However, just as the Bible prophesized, they will by and large be caught unprepared.

"But as the days of Noah were, so also will the coming of the Son of Man be. For as in the days before the flood, they were eating and drinking, marrying and giving in marriage, until the day that Noah entered into the ark, and did not realize until the flood came and took them all away, so also will the coming of the Son of Man be." Matthew 24:37-39

I've asked before where the pastors are who preach such things. Now I know that there are still some who do and I thank God for these preachers, but let us consider the times that we live in, let us consider it diligently. For this is not a time of carelessness or fun and games, but these are indeed very serious times that may very well in fact be the times right prior to the Rapture, where Christ comes to get His bride, the Church, those individuals who have truly repented and by faith believed into Jesus Christ as their Lord and Savior, accepting the free gift of Salvation.

"For by grace you are saved through faith; and that not of yourselves, it is the gift of God; not of works, that no one should boast." Ephesians 2:8-9

Like to hear it or not, a lot could be said and should be said about the times we are living in. I wrote before how truth has been cast down and on a daily basis I see that. Some news hits the headlines and one group says it isn't true, this is the truth, another group says it isn't true and that is the truth. Well the only thing to say in such situations, except for the sky is blue, it is daytime, it is nighttime, is the fact that the Bible, the Word of God (assuming it is not a perversion of God's Word, but a faithful translation like the King James version) is the ONLY ABSOLUTE TRUTH that we can be certain about in these days of darkness where men are stumbling around like the blind.

"And you shall know the truth, and the truth shall set you free." John 8:32

"Jesus said to him, I am the Way, the Truth, and the Life. No one comes to the Father except through Me." John 14:6

"The way of the wicked is as darkness; they do not know at what they stumble." Proverbs 4:19

I, like every other individual, will stand before my Creator one day. You will either stand at the Judgment Seat of Christ *(2 Cor. 5:10)*, where true Believers will be judged and see which of their works will not be consumed *(1 Cor. 3:13-15)* or you will stand at the Great White Throne Judgment, where you will be cast into the Lake of Fire for all eternity. There is the one line that people will gladly be last in.

"And I saw a great white throne and Him who sat on it, from whose face the earth and the heavens fled away. And there was found no place for them. And I saw the dead, small and great, standing before God. And books were opened. And another book was opened, which is the Book of Life. And the dead were judged according to their works, out of the things which were written in the books. And the sea gave up the dead who were in it, and Death and Hades delivered up the dead who were in them. And they were judged, each one, according to their works. And Death and Hades were cast into the Lake of Fire. This is the second death. And anyone not found written in the Book of Life was cast into the Lake of Fire." Revelation 20:11-15

All Will Stand is a ministry that points people towards God's truth, preaching repentance and remission of sins and Salvation thru faith in Jesus Christ. For, as has been pointed out regarding the following, which didn't believe? Was it the those who prophesied in Jesus's name, those who cast out demons in His name or those who did many works of power in His name?

"Not everyone who says to Me, Lord, Lord, will enter the kingdom of Heaven, but he who does the will of My Father in Heaven. Many will say to Me in that day, Lord, Lord, have we not prophesied in Your name, cast out demons in Your name, and done many works of

power in Your name? And then I will declare to them, I never knew you; depart from Me, you who work out lawlessness!" Matthew 7:21-23

Rather I say to you it was those who ignored Jesus's warning to repent.

Jesus said, *"I tell you, no; but unless you repent you will all likewise perish."* Luke 13:3

Shall I withhold the fact that there are many oddities between COVID-19 and preparing people for the mindset to obey the government and accept the mark of the beast? Shall I ignore that DARPA has a microchip that can be implanted coming out in 2021 that detects coronavirus? Should I ignore that there are people pushing for immunity certificates that require a vaccine or antibody test to resume life as normal?

While I am not saying that any of these things will happen for certainty or that even if they do that they will necessarily have anything to do with the mark of the beast that has been prophesized. I am saying that they are at minimum conditioning the masses for that sort of mindset. Think about it, being able to live normal under the guise of government permission. In a nutshell, if a man wants to buy or sell (live normal) they will be forced to take the mark of the beast.

"And he causes all, both small and great, rich and poor, free and slave, to receive a mark on their right hand or on their foreheads, so that no one may buy or sell except one who has the mark or the name of the beast, or the number of his name. Here is wisdom. Let him who has understanding calculate the number of the beast, for it is the number of a man, and his number is 666." Revelation 13:16-18

As a brief reminder, those who take the mark of the beast or worship the image of the beast are doomed to eternity in the Lake of Fire *(Rev. 20:4)*.

Now the same must be said regarding the things that are going on in the political theatre of this once great country (in terms of prosperity). For a great country would be one that by and large wholeheartedly truly serves God, not in pretense, but in actuality *(Jer. 3:10)*.

Should a Believer ignore God's Word in regarding prophecies of characteristics of the Antichrist? While it certainly is not our job to guess who the Antichrist is, nor would we even have the authority to do so, if a man is rising to power, should we then ignore it? Should we not at least warn men that something might be going on?! Should we not tell what God has made clear or look at a potential and tell others?

"Son of man, I have made you a watchman for the house of Israel; therefore hear the Word from My mouth, and give them warning from Me: When I say to the wicked, You shall die the death, and you give him no warning, nor speak to warn the wicked from his wicked way, to save his life, that same wicked man shall die in his iniquity; but his blood I will require at your hand. Yet, if you warn the wicked, and he does not turn from his wickedness, nor from his wicked way, he shall die in his iniquity; but you have delivered your soul. Again, when a righteous man turns from his righteousness and commits

iniquity, and I lay a stumbling block before him, he shall die. Because you did not give him warning, he shall die in his sin, and his righteousness which he has done shall not be remembered; but his blood I will require at your hand. Nevertheless if you warn the righteous man that the righteous should not sin, and he does not sin, he shall live life because he took warning; and you have delivered your soul." Revelation 3:17-21

This is not about guessing who the Antichrist is, as no one could possibly know for sure prior to the Rapture, but if there is a man rising to power who is matching what the Bible says, the only certain Truth that we have, then it should at least be noted. One, whether or not you want to, should at least acknowledge the fact that we ought to be watching and ready *(Matt. 24:42-44)*. If we are watching, should these things go unnoticed?

Why would God give characteristics of the Antichrist if they would not be useful?

"All Scripture is breathed by God, and is profitable for doctrine, for reproof, for correction, for instruction in righteousness, that the man of God may be complete, thoroughly equipped for every good work." 2nd Timothy 3:16-17

So, let's take a look and use it. Not to make a determination who the Antichrist is, but at least acknowledge that someone could be a suspect. My thoughts would make no one a suspect, but the Word of God and someone who matches these qualifications would make them a suspect. So therefore they would be a suspect based upon the Bible, based upon what God has spoken, not based upon any individual thoughts. Men have had a lot of suspects in times past regarding who the Antichrist might be, but these were often someone who simply had a characteristic or two, normally they would be someone who somehow was associated with the number 666, but if anyone would have taken the time to examine what the Bible actually teaches, they would have realized that according to God's Word, that person being named a suspect would have been sketchy at best.

Now there is a suspect, like it or not, who is rising to power and that suspect is President Donald Trump. He is a suspect, not because I say he is a suspect, but rather because of the characteristics of the Antichrist laid out in God's Word and the fact that he may very well match every single one of them. Once again, let me be very careful here, as I am by no means saying that President Donald Trump is the Antichrist, what I am saying is that he MUST be a suspect because he matches the characteristics or could very well match the characteristics that could be known prior to the *"time of Jacob's trouble" (Jer. 30:7)*. So according to what the Bible teaches, President Trump is a suspect.

I suspect that no one at the moment of this writing will listen. For those who are for President Trump often proclaim to be Christians and assume that President Trump is a Christian, another note on that in a moment. Then you have those who hate President Trump, but they also hate God's Word and therefore they would refuse to even look into such things.

Now, only furthering how President Trump could be a suspect, there is a long list of well known people who believe that President Trump is like the 'son of God', like Jesus Christ, like Moses, Elijah or one of the prophets or rather he is a man of God, being used of God.

Does a man of God own casinos? Does a man of God have relationships like he has? Does a man of God be involved in debauchery, without repenting? Yet President Trump would be a perfect example of a 'man of God' to those who are perishing in the lukewarm churches, those who go to these churches that refuse to preach repentance, who refuse to take following Jesus Christ as their Lord and Savior seriously. They refuse to be zealous for Christ, they refuse to pick up the Cross and carry on. These are the blind leading the blind and Jesus warned about such.

"Let them alone. They are blind leaders of the blind. And if the blind leads the blind, both will fall into the ditch." Matthew 15:14

Will these not be the ones who will believe the strong delusion sent by God? If not, which group will that be? Certainly not the godless, as they wouldn't match the description.

"For the mystery of lawlessness is already at work; only He is now restraining, until it is raised from out of the midst. And then the lawless one will be unveiled, whom the Lord will consume with the breath of His mouth and destroy with the brightness of His coming. The coming of the lawless one is according to the working of Satan, with all power, signs, and lying wonders, and with all unrighteous deception among those who are perishing, because they did not receive the love of the truth, that they might be saved. And for this reason God will send them strong delusion, that they should believe the lie, that they all may be judged who did not believe the truth but had pleasure in unrighteousness." 2nd Thessalonians 2:7-12

In January, prior to our world becoming some sort of scene out of a sci-fi movie, I published a book entitled *Repent! How, Even if, President Trump was the Antichrist the Church Wouldn't Know It.*

In that book I laid out what the Bible says about the Tribulation, the Rapture, I talked about the strong delusion sent by God and used President Trump as an example of how the Antichrist could be rising to power and the church wouldn't know it. Now I am going to lay out what the Bible says are characteristics of the Antichrist and point out how President Trump MUST be a suspect, because he seemingly matches every single one that could possibly be known beforehand, every single one.

Before we dive into that discussion, I will discuss what I hope would happen if the end is near.

Much has been said recently about potentially election mayhem. However, I have been discussing such things privately for months prior to anyone else declaring such things recently about what could happen after the election. Now these are just some 'thoughts' about what -could- happen. I certainly don't have any special revelation and do not know what the future holds, but if these things occurred, which is certainly plausible, I would hope that this would open a window to allow people to look behind the curtain, see that something is not right, question it and perhaps seek God with there whole heart, repent and believe into Jesus Christ as their Savior prior to the Rapture. Though as far as I know, this article may never even get published prior to the Rapture happening.

Due to having read and studied the Bible for years, I could see the possibility of God providing a last chance for people to repent. For I strongly believe that the false church, which is predominant in the United States, will believe the lie, for God will send them strong delusion. I don't believe this is true with most Catholics, though also a false pagan religion, it is different as a more pagan works-based religion, one where the thoughts of Salvation are not so much as repeating a prayer and pretending to be Saved, but rather having to do with rites and rituals. Time will tell how that works out, but by then it will be too late.

This election is setup to be a disaster. I had wrote some articles years ago about whether or not everything with President Trump was a deception of biblical proportions, things just seemed off. I have watched and carefully evaluated things that have happened in comparison to the Bible. Now it seems that whether or not President Trump wins the next election, he is going to stay in power.

The ground work, perhaps a large deception as the best deception has measures of truth to it, has been laid that even if he loses he will still win, because it will have been a fraudulent election and the courts will rule in his favor. Without getting into what may or may not be the details of such an ordeal, one must consider that if this happens we will have a large potential problem on our hands. Let's also consider that President Trump is a suspect of being the Antichrist, not based upon my thinking, but, as you will see, based upon the characteristics that have been prophesized in the Bible.

Now we have already had many cities with burning buildings, lootings and mass chaos, this with a pandemic that is to those who can see a sham. While I am not going to throw the baby out with the bath water, as they say, truly the numbers show that COVID-19 is only somewhat more dangerous than the average flu. Clearly what has happened is a government overreach of power around the world, of which I have seen abuses of power and a dystopian style government in many parts of the world, including here in the United States.

Should some precautions be taken? Sure, but not nearly at the level of which they are, our world has been turned upside down and this under President Trump's watch. Whether the coronavirus is manufactured in a lab or a natural event (seemingly unlikely due to some of what I have studied), makes no difference, as either way it is being used as a weapon against we the people, even against God by limited those who preach the Gospel.

In fact, I even have a friend who thought to start taking his family to church, but due to COVID he didn't want to go. Now is the time people need to be fearing God and seeking Him before it is too late. If only pastors would take as serious the things of God as our government does this so-called pandemic!

Now if President Trump does use the court system to 'steal' rightfully so or not the election, just how do you think the left will react given the recent ongoings in places like Portland, Oregon? I see the headlines and it ranges from mass civil unrest to civil war.

If you supposedly were always lerious of the government (rightfully so!), have you who had taken the red pill now been blue pilled? For those who always thought martial law was coming and they were getting prepared for it (probably still do regarding the potential civil unrest), of which I am no stranger of such things, do you now listen to the pundits who are pushing Trump as the Savior of the Republic? Do you not see? Why are you so blind?

Nonetheless that blindness only furthers what I have always called the conspiracy of all conspiracies and that is that this so-called new world order is simply the Antichrist world government that is behind the scenes slowly rising to power, being held back until it is in God's timing *(2 Th. 2:7; 2 Pet. 3:9)*. The ultimate conspiracy is the distraction of such things, for the same people who at least used to talk about underground tunnels, railways, FEMA camps, you name it, are now on the Trump train?! Just where is this Trump train going? Auschwitz?

The reality has never been the people verses shadow government but rather the god of this world...Satan...verses God the Creator of each of us. The solution has already been provided by God and that solution was that Jesus died on the Cross for our sins, that we might be Saved.

"For God so loved the world that He gave His only begotten Son, that everyone believing into Him should not perish but have eternal life. For God did not send His Son into the world to judge the world, but that the world through Him might be saved. The one believing into Him is not judged; but the one not believing is judged already, because he has not believed in the name of the only begotten Son of God. And this is the judgment, that the Light has come into the world, and men loved darkness rather than the Light, for their deeds were evil. For everyone practicing evil hates the Light and does not come to the Light, lest his deeds should be reproved. But the one doing the truth comes to the Light, that his deeds may be clearly seen, that they have been worked in God." John 3:16-21

"But God demonstrates His own love toward us, in that while we were yet sinners, Christ died for us." Romans 5:8

In order to accept that free gift one must repent and by faith believe into Jesus Christ as their Lord and Savior, irregardless of whether or not you believe there are some, numerous or no conspiracies against we the people. I assure you in order for the *"time of*

Jacob's trouble" (Jer. 30:7), better known as the Tribulation to be true, there certainly is a new world order or Antichrist government behind the scenes.

"For we do not wrestle against flesh and blood, but against rulers, against authorities, against the world's rulers of the darkness of this age, against spiritual wickedness in the heavenlies." Ephesians 6:12

So my hope, not knowing, but my hope is that if the end is near that God will allow the blind to snap out of their blindness and at least briefly consider what is going on behind the scenes. That they might look behind the curtain and see that not is all that it seems. Even if they don't fully understand the Bible or know only the basics, that they would have an opportunity to be able to repent before it is too late. For many people proclaim the name of Christ in this country, but few of them are actually Saved.

"Enter by the narrow gate; for wide is the gate and broad is the way that leads to destruction, and there are many entering in through it. Because narrow is the gate and distressing is the way which leads unto life, and there are few who find it. Beware of false prophets, who come to you in sheep's clothing, but inwardly they are ravenous wolves. You will know them from their fruits. Do men gather grapes from thornbushes or figs from thistles? Even so, every good tree produces excellent fruit, but a corrupt tree produces evil fruit. A good tree is not able to produce evil fruit, nor is a corrupt tree able to produce excellent fruit. Every tree that does not produce excellent fruit is cut down and thrown into the fire. Therefore from their fruits you will know them. Not everyone who says to Me, Lord, Lord, will enter the kingdom of Heaven, but he who does the will of My Father in Heaven. Many will say to Me in that day, Lord, Lord, have we not prophesied in Your name, cast out demons in Your name, and done many works of power in Your name? And then I will declare to them, I never knew you; depart from Me, you who work out lawlessness!" Matthew 7:13-23

So if this country descends further into chaos and the Rapture hasn't yet happened, the only logical response would be for President Trump to declare hot martial law via the Insurrection Act. He has already threatened to use that old legislation that is still on the books. Now I say this not in support because I believe based on the Bible that President Trump is a suspect to being the Antichrist.

Therefore, I know that the Antichrist will be the biggest deceiver that has ever lived. If that is the case then certainly this whole thing will have been a deception of biblical proportions and President Trump will have unleashed a genius plot (another characteristic *Da. 8:23*) of dividing the country and will likely manage to maintain overall support even during a martial law scenario as his supporters will believe he is fighting the deep state and trying to restore America (of which he would still probably be successful in doing so). Likely there would be numerous deaths at first, but afterwards when martial law hit eventually order and prosperity (perhaps via payments from the FEDCoin they are trying to pass).

Have we not been prepped for martial law? Have we not now been conditioned to accept travel restrictions, personal liberty restrictions, etc.? Why? Do we not, at least to a logical person, have the evidence that it was total overkill in the supposed fight against COVID?

If, at my last check, 43% of all deaths from COVID were in nursing or assistance living homes, then why was the advice and warning that I offered months ago regarding this not thought of by our elected leaders, some of who became mini-dictators? That advice was simple. As it was known early on that COVID caused a much higher rate of death in our elderly people than younger, why not have used the National Guard to provide all of the nursing and care for people in these homes?

These trained soldiers could have been assigned active duty providing assistance and care for those who were most at high risk. There could have been RV's or tents put up for them, food provided as they lived on site, not leaving, so that the risk of infection would have been minimal, compared to the nurses and other workers who worked a shift, had a possibility of getting infected and then returned to work, possibly bringing COVID with them.

Those workers could have been laid off and given full pay, providing only a minimal impact on the economy and saving numerous lives. After all we were told this was about saving lives, what about that!!! Instead numerous small business owners went out of business, spent thousands on nonsense, many tens of millions of people were laid off. Suicides skyrocketed and drug & alcohol abuse went through the roof. What type of dystopia do we live in?

Now the worse, unless those behind the scenes want to tell us that it mixed with the influenza and is now more deadly or a new more deadly strain is released on the public, the worse should be behind us...though I don't count on it. Even in Australia they are treating people as if it is Nazi Germany in order to help stop the 'spread' and keep people safe. Last I checked, the amount of government overreach there is so out of touch with reality, it was saddening. Same could be said in many countries around the world.

So, if the end is near, the normalcy of our life is probably not ever going to return to a complete normal, in fact it will just become more and more bizarre. I wonder if this is the lie that is spoken about in 2 Thessalonians 2:11, considering the blind supporters of Trump who chose to ignore the obvious red flag of the Israel peace plan that he is making huge progress on, a sure sign and probably the best that was given as a guaranteed suspect of someone being the Antichrist...more on that in a bit.

Perhaps if the nation goes into more chaos, people will get a peek behind the curtain and their willful or purposeful *(2 Cor. 4:3-4)* blindness will allow them a brief chance to repent and accept Christ as their Savior. Most people believe in Jesus, they believe they are Saved, but they have refused to repent.

Could this be the reason our government is trying to pass legislation that would allow direct payments from the Federal Reserve via some bond scheme to American's bank accounts. Are things justifiably that bad at the moment or is it as Mike Pompeo said, a live exercise, indicating that worse is yet to come. Pompeo stated the following:

"We will continue to fight these battles, it is a never ending struggle... until the Rapture."

"As a Christian I certainly believe that's possible," Pompeo responded when asked whether Trump is a new Esther, who in the Bible convinced the king of Persia not to slaughter the Jewish people." -- TheHill.com 3/21/19

Now let's take a look once more at the Antichrist characteristics that the Bible says and align why President Trump must be a suspect for being the Antichrist. This is not to discourage support of President Trump, but Believers should at least be aware of the facts, be watching and ready, not ignorant of the fact that the end may be near.

"He shall not regard the God of his fathers, nor the desire of women; nor regard any god. For he shall magnify himself above them *all." Daniel 11:37*

In another article, that was compiled into the book *Repent; How, Even if, President Trump was the Antichrist the Church Wouldn't Know It*, I go over the fact that I think people who assume the Antichrist must be gay are mistaken. What should be mentioned here is the *"God of his fathers"* which would indicate that the Antichrist must be Jewish.

President Trump's parents both died at the Long Island Jewish Medical Center. In fact in Donald Trump's book *The Art of the Deal* he claims that his grandfather was from Sweden, in fact he was from Germany. His father, Fred Christ Trump was well known for being heavily involved in Jewish circles, as well as advisors to Donald Trump, like Roy Cohn.

Digging through President Trump's genealogy one finds that there are numerous Jewish surnames. In fact a lot of these details have been scrubbed, including a once reference to his parents dying at the Long Island Jewish Medical Center. There is ample evidence to prove that President Trump likely has a Jewish lineage. In fact, many rabbis in Israel also think so.

My friend and the other person behind the All Will Stand ministry did some research. He found that many rabbis thought President Trump might be the Messiah or at least paving the way for the Messiah. (Their thoughts are the Messiah is simply a political leader who restores Israel to it's rightful place, not as Americans think in regards to the Antichrist.) In fact a group of prominent rabbis traveled to Europe because they believe they could trace President Trump's lineage to king David. What they found was never made known.

So why is this important? Like President Trump, I also have lineage connecting myself to the tribe of Judah from the diaspora in Germany. In fact, when I researched my genealogy I found that many of the great-great names of the past were Enoch, etc., all Jewish biblical names. That all changed quickly, once my family integrated in the United States. However, there is a large anti-Semitic movement around the world.

Just mentioning that it appears that President Trump is our first Jewish President, will get people asking if you don't like Jews. Certainly that is not the case, as I love the Jewish people, as God's chosen people *(Duet. 7:6)*. Though I am not ignorant of the things that go on behind the scenes. I have seen the Freemasonry symbolism of the Knesset and it is quite obvious, just like the occultic symbolism that is riddled throughout famous landmarks in the United States as well.

So why does this matter? The unfortunate truth is a lot of the patriotic movement who see a conspiracy in many things, also believe that the Jews are behind these conspiracies. In fact this viewpoint is even more prevalent in Europe than in the United States. They point to Hollywood, the banking industry, etc., all being controlled by Jews and they also believe that the elite are Jewish or crypto-Jews. So they have a distrust of the Jewish people.

So even if certain Jewish people are behind such things as the Federal Reserve scheme, that doesn't neglect them from being God's chosen people. In fact *"the time of Jacob's trouble" (Jer. 30:7)*, better known as the Tribulation, is about the restoration of the Jewish people. In the end they will realize that Jesus is their Messiah and God will restore them giving them new hearts.

"And I will pour on the house of David, and on the inhabitants of Jerusalem, the Spirit of grace and supplication. And they shall look on Me whom they have pierced; and they shall mourn for Him, as one mourns for an only son, *and* they *shall be bitter over Him, like the bitterness over the firstborn." Zechariah 12:10*

"Furthermore He said to me, Son of man, do you see what they are doing, the great abominations that the house of Israel commits here, to make Me go far away from My sanctuary? Now turn again, you will see greater abominations. So He brought me to the door of the court; and when I looked, behold, a hole in the wall. Then He said to me, Son of man, dig into the wall; and when I dug into the wall, there was an opening. And He said to me, Go in, and see the evil abominations which they do there. So I went in and saw; and behold, every sort of creeping thing, abominable beasts, and all the idols of the house of Israel, carved all around on the wall. And there stood before them seventy men of the elders of the house of Israel, and in their midst stood Jaazaniah the son of Shaphan. Each man had a censer in his hand, and a thick cloud of incense went up. Then He said to me, Son of man, have you seen what the elders of the house of Israel do in the dark, every man in the room of his idols? For they say, Jehovah does not see us, Jehovah has forsaken the land. And He said to me, Turn again, and you will see greater abominations that they are doing. So He brought me to the door of the north gate of the house of Jehovah; and behold, women were sitting there weeping for Tammuz. Then He said to me, Have you seen this, O son of man? Turn again, you will see greater abominations than these. So He brought me into the inner court of the house of Jehovah; and behold,

at the door of the temple of Jehovah, between the porch and the altar, were about twenty-five men with their backs toward the temple of Jehovah and their faces toward the east, and they were bowing down to the sun toward the east. And He said to me, Have you seen this, O son of man? Is it a trivial thing to the house of Judah to commit the abominations which they commit here? For they have filled the land with violence; then they have returned to provoke Me to anger. Indeed they put the branch to their nose. Therefore I also will act in fury. My eye will not spare nor will I have pity; and though they cry in My ears with a loud voice, I will not hear them." Ezekiel 8:6-18

"I will also give you a new heart and put a new spirit within you; I will take the heart of stone out of your flesh and give you a heart of flesh." Ezekiel 36:26

What is odd is that the mainstream media who has dug up every single piece of dirt on President Trump that they could, somehow can not find out that he is also likely Jewish. Now with all of the anti-Semitism that is out there in the world, it would seem very hard for President Trump to have the full support of the patriots in this country or be well liked throughout Europe if it was known that he was Jewish. Yet in Israel President Trump is absolutely loved and respected.

This would seemingly pave the way to allow President Trump, if he were the Antichrist, to be known as Jewish to the inner circles of Israel's leaders and important religious people, the only people who would matter if they ended up declaring him the Messiah. This would also prevent those who would be suspicious of such things in other parts of the world, including the United States from withdrawing full support of President Trump being the leader of the movement to go after the elite and deep state.

Now prior to President Trump, famous talk show hosts and internet news outlets that provided non-stop news coverage about a conspiracy against the American people, including martial law, taking away our guns, etc., have now become nonstop Trump train peddlers.

Despite the fact that President Trump's comments helped to cause red flag laws and that he may very well use the Insurrection Act (hot martial law) after a contested election, this doesn't even raise an eyebrow in the Trump supporting circles. More could be said, as how the NAFTA replacement is essentially the same as NAFTA, but seemingly President Trump can do no wrong.

Just as President Trump had tear gas and rubber bullets used outside of St. John's Church in Washington, D.C., so that he could take a quick picture holding up a Bible, those who call themselves Christians are seemingly blind to any possibility that he could potentially be a wolf in sheep's clothing. Everything that was ever warned about by the alternative media in regarding a conspiracy against the American people is now null and void with President Trump in power. His constituents trust him and quite obviously the left has gone so far that they have no choice but to vote for him.

So the fact that it appears that President Trump is our first Jewish President does not make him a suspect for being the Antichrist, though the lack of public knowledge regarding such things certainly does raise an eyebrow. Looking at biblical prophecy, what must make him a suspect is the fact that he is working on a peace deal with Israel. When you add in the Jewish prospect, that makes it even the more interesting.

"And he shall confirm a covenant with many for one week. And in the middle of the week he shall cause the sacrifice and the grain offering to cease. And on a corner will be abominations that cause horror, even until the end. And that which was decreed shall be poured out on the desolate." Daniel 9:27

Only the first part of this verse *"And he shall confirm a covenant with many for one week."* can be used to provide evidence of someone being an Antichrist suspect. The rest of it will not be fulfilled until after the Rapture has happened and the world has been plunged into the Tribulation.

Now the Bible has laid out this as one of the characteristics of knowing who the Antichrist is. This is not to suggest that who the Antichrist is would be known before the Rapture, for quite clearly the Bible teaches otherwise.

"Let no one deceive you by any means; for that Day will not come unless the falling away comes first, and the man of sin is unveiled, the son of perdition, who opposes and exalts himself above all that is called God or that is honored, so that he sits as God in the temple of God, declaring of himself that he is God. Do you not remember that when I was still with you I told you these things? And now you know what is restraining, that he may be unveiled in his own time. For the mystery of lawlessness is already at work; only He is now restraining, until it is raised from out of the midst. And then the lawless one will be unveiled, whom the Lord will consume with the breath of His mouth and destroy with the brightness of His coming." 2nd Thessalonians 2:3-8

Yet there will rise a man who is the Antichrist and one of the things that he WILL do is have a peace treaty with Israel. So by definition, anyone who is working on a peace deal with Israel, whether Vladimir Putin or Donald Trump, must be a suspect. This is not according to my thoughts, but what the Bible has clearly prophesied. The Bible would list that person as a suspect.

Now no one would know if this is the peace deal that is the one prophesied in the Bible or simply a different deal. As I cautioned previously, people also ought not to take and watch this deal assuming that they can postpone seeking God after they see evidence of the Bible being true. (As if there wasn't ample evidence everywhere one looks, they refuse to have 'eyes that see'.!) For past deals were done in secret prior and then unveiled to the public afterwards for a ceremony. The President Clinton deal is an example of that.

When you consider President Trump's wild support from Israel, it only adds to the fact that he being a suspect should be taken seriously, regardless of the Trump train mentality.

..."the Jewish people love [Trump] … like he's the King of Israel. They love him like he is the second coming of God." -- Wayne Allyn Root

President Trump has commented about the importance of an Israeli peace plan.

"We want to create peace between Israel and the Palestinians. We will get it done," Trump said. *"We will be working so hard to get it done. I think there is a very good chance and I think we will."* -- President Trump

"It is something that I think is frankly, maybe, not as difficult as people have thought over the years." -- President Trump

"That's the ultimate deal," Trump said. *"As a deal maker, I'd like to do … the deal that can't be made. And do it for humanity's sake."* -- President Trump

"I've had a lot of, actually, great Israeli businesspeople tell me, you can't do that, it's impossible," Trump said. *"I disagree, I think you can make peace. I think people are tired now of being shot, killed. At some point, when do they come? I think we can do that. I have reason to believe I can do that."* -- President Trump

President Trump refers to the Israeli peace deal as the *"deal of the century"*. Now a lot of people have tried to make a lasting peace deal with Israel and have all failed. Yet people who have tried before have been immediately accused of being the Antichrist, President Clinton is a prime example of this.

There were a ton of so-called evangelical christians who didn't just name President Clinton as a suspect to being the Antichrist, but flat out said that he was the Antichrist because of a peace deal that he had reached with Israel. In fact a lot went even further and stretched the six year peace deal that was inked to a seven year deal, calling it 'the peace deal' and stating that we were in the Tribulation, based upon the false notion that the Rapture happens at the end of the Tribulation.

This was back in 2000 and it is quite obvious that the Tribulation did not happen, yet there were many loud mouths who were proclaiming that the Tribulation had started, despite the fact that the 'starting gun' the Rapture did not occur.

Numerous people went around on a then newer notion of the internet proclaiming that Bill Clinton was the Antichrist. Well he isn't and was not. If he were, the Rapture would have happened and the *"time of Jacob's trouble" (Jer. 30:7)* would have began. This was back in the era of the Left Behind movie and book popularizing the notion of a Rapture and Tribulation to come.

Then Churches would still preach on such things, but when the year 2000 came they seemed to give up.

"Beloved, I now write to you this second epistle (in both of which I stir up your pure minds by way of reminder), that you may remember the words which were spoken before by the holy prophets, and the commandment of us, the apostles of the Lord and Savior, knowing this first: that scoffers will come in the last days, walking according to their own lusts, and saying, Where is the promise of His coming? For since the fathers fell asleep, all things continue as they were since the beginning of creation. For of this they are willfully ignorant: that by the Word of God the heavens were of old, and the earth standing out of water and in the water, by which the world that then existed perished, being flooded with water. But the heavens and the earth which are now preserved by the same Word, are reserved for fire until the day of judgment and destruction of ungodly men. But, beloved, do not be unaware of this one thing, that with the Lord one day is as a thousand years, and a thousand years as one day. The Lord is not slow concerning His promise, as some count slowness, but is longsuffering toward us, not purposing that any should perish but that all should come to repentance. But the day of the Lord will come as a thief in the night, in which the heavens will pass away with a loud noise, and the elements will be dissolved with intense burning; both the earth and the works that are in it will be burned up." 2nd Peter 3:1-10

Apparently the year 2000 and going off of these verses:

"But, beloved, do not be unaware of this one thing, that with the Lord one day is as a thousand years, and a thousand years as one day." 2nd Peter 3:8

"After two days He will restore us to life. In the third day He will raise us up, and we shall live in His presence." Hosea 6:2

However, obviously the date is not the same as we think. All of these things will happen in God's timing, not man's supposed understanding of such things. Now fast forward to 2020 and a lot has changed.

Now Churches, even independent fundamental Baptist Churches, rarely talk about such things, despite the fact that we are to be watching and ready.

"Watch therefore, for you do not know what hour your Lord comes. But know this, that if the master of the house had known what hour the thief comes, he would have watched and not allowed his house to be dug through. Therefore you also be ready, for the Son of Man comes at an hour you do not expect." Matthew 24:42-44

Have they given up? Has the notion become unpopular and unbelievable? What has happened?

Certainly the apostasy is in full bloom, one of the reasons that these things are happening, but shouldn't a peace deal being worked on by President Trump, a man who gets things done, the basis for his popularity, be noted by those who are preaching from the pulpits?

Do we ignore now what the Bible teaches regarding a peace deal with Israel and the Antichrist, just because President Trump is popular and considered a man of God or a man used by God? Do we ignore a clear prophecy regarding the Antichrist just because the Democrats are so bad, Trump must be good? Do we ignore the fact that even if we fully support our 'christian' President who is supposedly working on behalf of God and fighting the evil, that he also is matching a description of the Antichrist, one that does make him a suspect of being the Antichrist, based from the Bible, not from private opinion? I think we should not, I think it should be at least noted.

A certain amount of skepticism about the world in which we live and our popular leader, President Trump, should remain as he is a suspect for being the Antichrist, due to the possibility that he will achieve a peace deal with Israel and that could be the deal that is prophesied in the Bible. We MUST remember this and not fully trust him, even if we support him. For to ignore such a fact is certainly evidence of not 'watching and being ready'.

When I was considering these things, I noted that the verse actually says *"And he shall confirm a covenant __with many__ for one week."* Let's take a quick look at that.

President Clinton's treaty was essentially just between Israel and the so-called Palestine people. Yet the Bible clearly states that not only is the peace deal for seven years (one week), but is it with many.

President Trump says that 7-9 countries are involved with his peace deal with Israel, for those who believe the Bible, one should take note. Not only is President Trump trying to get a peace deal with Israel, but with 7-9 countries the fact that the 'covenant' is with many only adds to the reasons that he must be a suspect of being the Antichrist.

In fact when the recent recognition of Israel from the United Arab Emirates, President Trump was nominated for a Nobel Peace prize. This is how amazing it was that he was able to pull off such an unimaginable thing in the Middle East.

Consider that President Trump pulled out of the Iran deal. Now Iran has been working even harder on producing nuclear weapons, threatening not only Israel, but the entire power structure of the Middle East. Could it be that President Trump pulled out of that deal, not because it was necessarily a bad deal, but in order to force other countries to get onboard of his peace deal??? Could he be using the mutual threat of Iran against other countries like Saudi Arabia and the UAE as leverage, selling them weapons and technology in exchange for peace with Israel???

Recently Sudan accused the United States of adding another term before they can be removed from the terror watchlist of countries. While Sudan was apparently working hard to ensure they met the requirements to be removed from such a designation, now the only requirement is to make peace with Israel, something that originally was not included. This is their accusation against our country. So the theory that the Iran deal removal might be being used a leverage is not so far fetched.

Whether or not President Trump gets reelected or if the peace deal proceeds or if this is the peace deal that is prophesied in the Bible makes little difference. Until these things are known, as long as there is a realistic prospect for peace and I think that Trump supporters could agree that Trump gets stuff done, there will remain the fact that President Trump must be a suspect of being the Antichrist, whether or not one wants to acknowledge that.

Let me simply add here as another reminder, as I have done in both the book and the articles that are available on All Will Stand's website, I am NOT saying that President Trump is the Antichrist, no one can say that. What I am simply saying is that President Trump must be a suspect, not based upon any personal opinion, but based upon what the Bible prophesizes about the coming Antichrist. Simply put, one thing we can know beforehand is that the Antichrist will be working on a peace deal and be involved in that peace deal -- that is a fact. Therefore anyone involved with such things, irregardless, must be a suspect. How much more so for those who are likely Jewish, popular and seemingly matching potentially every single characteristic that the Bible lays out regarding the Antichrist?

In closing this article, which I would consider to be an additional chapter to the book, I am going to look at one more characteristic. A few were mentioned in the book and quotes were given. A lot of these I will not go into detail, because I can't. No one is going to fully know what they mean until during the Tribulation and at that point if you were Left Behind, you were Left Behind.

The time to ensure that you are right with God, that you have truly repented and by faith believed into Jesus Christ as your Lord and Savior is now.

"And also through his cunning he will cause deceit to prosper in his hand." Daniel 8:25a

One characteristic of the Antichrist is that he will be a deceiver. In fact there will never have been a man who is a greater deceiver than he is, because his power comes from Satan, who is the father of lies *(John 8:44)*.

Not only is the Antichrist a deceiver but *"he will cause deceit to prosper in his hand"*. This is serious, not only is he deceiving but his deception works. I had wrote an article called *Truth Cast Down*, another characteristic of the Antichrist *(Da. 8:25)*. I can only point to President Trump calling everything fake news, etc., as even further reason to take him being a suspect seriously. So what does this mean?

What this means is that even if President Trump were the Antichrist, people are not going to see it. For if the Antichrist is able to cause deceit to prosper in his hand, this means that his followers are going to believe his lies. In my opinion, this is exactly what I see having happened and how I see that people could believe the 'strong delusion' *(2 Thes. 2:11)* that God sends them, essentially believing the lie.

Now I certainly can not know these things for sure and neither can anyone else. The world will be caught off guard when the Rapture happens and whoever the Antichrist may be will have been able to have deceit prosper in his hand, essentially people will believe his deception. This only adds to the equation.

Now, it is not our job to determine who the Antichrist is, but I think it is reasonable to remind people of how serious of a time this is in the world's history. I think it is important that we are 'watching and ready' and that those who are doing the Lord's work be found so doing when He comes.

"Blessed is that servant whom his master, when he comes, will find so doing." Matthew 24:46

Nonetheless for those naysayers who say such a thing should not be said, I hope you are not one of the many churches, including Baptist, who are holding mini-rallies during your preaching. For if you do not like this preaching of pointing this out and you say that our focus should not be on this (I agree), but you also tell your congregation in a few less words than actually saying to vote for Trump, I would also tell you the same, our focus shouldn't be on politics. So do not have two sets of standards.

"Therefore you are without excuse, O man, whoever you are who judges, for in whatever you judge another you condemn yourself; for you who judge practice the same things." Romans 2:1

Then again if one were to study exactly what the Two Witnesses do during the Tribulation it should be abundantly clear that most do not believe them until after they are killed and resurrected.

"And I will give to my two witnesses, and they will prophesy one thousand two hundred and sixty days, clothed in sackcloth. These are the two olive trees and the two lampstands standing before the God of the earth. And if anyone tries to harm them, fire proceeds from their mouth and devours their enemies. And if anyone tries to harm them, he must be killed in this manner. These have authority to shut the heavens, so that no rain falls in the days of their prophecy; and they have authority over waters to turn them to blood, and to strike the earth with every plague, as often as they desire. And when they finish their testimony, the beast that ascends out of the bottomless pit will make war against them, overcome them, and kill them. And their dead bodies will lie in the street of the great city which spiritually is called Sodom and Egypt, where also our Lord was crucified. And those from the peoples, tribes, tongues, and nations will see their dead bodies three and a half days, and not allow their dead bodies to be put into graves. And those who dwell on the earth will rejoice over them, make merry, and send gifts to one another, because these two prophets tormented those who dwell on the earth. And after three and a half days the spirit of life from God entered into them, and they stood on their feet, and great terror fell on those who saw them. And they heard a loud voice out of Heaven saying to them, Come up here. And they ascended towards Heaven in a cloud, and their enemies saw them." Revelation 11:3-12

What, aside from telling people to repent, do you think they are going to be talking about. Most likely they will be telling people that they are in the Tribulation and that would include naming with authority given by God who the Antichrist is. So if it were that obvious during the first half of the Tribulation who the Antichrist was, there would be no reason for people not to believe whatever they were speaking. Just what exactly that means and thoughts on that I will keep to myself. Just do not be the one who finds out in person on the earth, but rather find yourself having been Raptured, watching these things unfold with Christ.

Amen!

www.ingramcontent.com/pod-product-compliance
Lightning Source LLC
Chambersburg PA
CBHW032115280326
41933CB00009B/852